I0233625

Mysterious Joy

CARL HOEFLER

Sermons for
Lent and Easter

CYCLE C FIRST LESSON TEXTS
FROM THE COMMON LECTIONARY

C.S.S. Publishing Co., Inc.

Lima, Ohio

MYSTERIOUS JOY

Copyright © 1988 by
The C.S.S. Publishing Company, Inc.
Lima, Ohio

All rights reserved. No part of this publication may be reproduced, stored in a retrieval system, or transmitted in any form or by any means, electronic, mechanical, photocopying, recording, or otherwise, without the prior permission of the publisher. Inquiries should be addressed to: The C.S.S. Publishing Company, Inc., 628 South Main Street, Lima, Ohio 45804.

Library of Congress Cataloging-in-Publication Data

Hoefler, Richard Carl, 1922 -
  Mysterious joy.

  1. Lenten sermons. 2. Easter — Sermons. 3. Ascension Day — Sermons. 4. Sermons, American. I. Common lectionary. II. Title.

BV4277.H56 1988   252'.62   88-2576
ISBN 1-55673-059-4

8856 / ISBN 1-55673-059-4
PRINTED IN U.S.A.

Table of Contents

Dedicated to my mother,
who brought great joy
into my life and into
the lives of many others.

Rejoice! It's Lent

Rejoice! It's Lent. Sounds strange doesn't it? Joy and Lent just do not seem to go together. Lent is the somber season. In popular practice Lent possesses all the marks of a six-week funeral. The paraments are the deep purple of a dowager's dress. Hallelujahs are silenced within the service of the liturgy. Social celebrations are cancelled — or at least curtailed. Our attention is focused exclusively on the crucified body of a young man dying in agony on a criminal's cross. Our emotions are moved to tears by such words as suffering, sacrifice, passion, and death. All of this emphasis on the cross is intended to drive us to repentance and to acts of fasting.

This Lenten emphasis on the death and suffering of our Lord is not only a distortion of the biblical witness and the practice of the primitive church, it is also a destructive division of the theology of redemption. Originally the intent of Lent was to provide a period of meditation and contemplation in preparation for the Christian Pascha [Passover] which celebrated the crucifixion and the resurrection as one single redemptive event.

Today, however, we have torn asunder what God had originally joined together. Easter for most of us has been reduced to a single Sunday; whereas, the one day called "Good Friday" has been expanded and intensified into a forty-day deathwatch called "Lent." The number of days in the Lenten Season have grown like barnacles to the ship of the church as it moved through the history of liturgical observances.

Four facts confront us concerning Lent. First, our Lord did not establish it; the church did. Second, in the early church, before Holy Week, before Holy Thursday and Good Friday came into regular liturgical usage, the preparation for Easter was the Great Vigil. Two preceding day's of fasting and prayer were incumbent upon every Christian. These forty hours grew to become a forty-day observance. Third, as Lent grew in length, it changed from a practice of meditation and contemplation of both the crucifixion and the resurrection to a forty-day period of penitence and remorse related exclusively to our Lord's passion and death; thereby, it became simply an extension of the mood and character of Good Friday. Fourth, the resurrection was divorced from the crucifixion and a truncated theology of Lent was conceived and developed in the minds of Christians. The Lenten practices, which resulted from this truncated theology, were and are illegitimate.

In the light of all this, how should we observe Lent this year? What is our proper attitude in this holy season? In an attempt to find some directives, let us look at the First Lesson for today. Here, we find the prophet Joel standing at the doorway to Lent. Joel is one of the minor prophets. His book is only three chapters long. You could quickly thumb through the Bible and miss the book of Joel altogether. Although Joel is a little book, it is a giant in its grasp of the Old Testament concept of God's faithfulness in fulfilling his promises.

Joel begins his prophecy by describing a devastating plague of locusts. Then, he moves to a glorious promise of restoration. At the center of his message Joel cries out, "Repent," an appropriate word for Lent. But, just as we do not always understand the meaning of Lent, we frequently fail to understand the meaning of the word "repent."

When we hear the word "repent," we immediately conjure up visions of sackcloth and ashes, tear-stained faces of guilty sinners filled with remorse, sorrow and regret crying out in their misery for the mercy of God. Now, sorrow and regret are certainly a part of the process of repentance in the Bible; but, they are not the main elements in the process.

The basic thrust of the word "repent" is the call to God's chosen people to turn — to return to God. Like a drillmaster's shout, "About face!"; so, repentance is a sharp command given to turn and return to God. It is a call to turn our entire life in the direction of God. However, within the command itself, there is a reminder that the one, who gives the command, is a God who has never turned away from his people. There-fore, repentance is not a "put-down." In truth, it is an "up-lift." We are to repent not primarily because *we* have done something bad or wrong; but, because *our God* has done some-thing very *good* and will do something even *better* in the future.

When one reads all three chapters of Joel, it is apparent that this prophet is not chiding or criticizing, nor is he con-demning or even judging the people. Rather, his concern is to comfort the distress in the hearts of the people as they face the desolation of their land. A plague of locusts has devastated the land. Like an armed force of invaders with teeth as sharp as those of a lion, they have destroyed the grapevines, chewed up the fig trees and the olive trees. The fields are bare. The very ground mourns. Joel adds, "the joy of the people is gone."

From the depths of despair Joel rises to the heights of joy. As his first words singe our ears with the fiery descriptions of desolation, his final words warm our hearts with a glori-ous hymn of promise and renewal. The day of the Lord is com-ing. What a day it will be! When the Lord comes, sickles will glisten in the sunlight as they cut the ripe wheat. Barns will bulge with abundant grain. Wine will flow from the moun-tains and milk from the hills. A fountain will spring forth in the middle of the house of the Lord and the people will feast and want no more.

Joel does not stop here with his prediction of material bless-ings. He goes on to the heights of spiritual ecstasy. When the Lord comes, he will pour out his Spirit on all flesh. Sons and daughters will prophesy. Old men will dream dreams and young men will see visions.

It is true that Joel states that the people fast, weep, and mourn in their state of desolation and depression; but, this is not so much a demand of what the people are to do as it is a description of what the people are currently doing. Could people survive the terrible invasion of locusts and the devastating drought that Joel describes without mourning, weeping, and tearing their clothes in despair? Joel was a realist. He saw the devastation of the land and the distress of the people. But, Joel was, at the same time, a man of vision. He saw beyond the tragic circumstances of his times to the day when God would fulfill his promises, restore the land, and bless the people.

Repent. Come back to God. God is kind and full of mercy. God is patient with his people and he keeps his promises. God is always willing to forgive and not to punish his people. God gives and God takes away; but God in the end, returns all things to his people. This is the joy of Lent, the vision of victory in the midst of defeat — the vision of forgiveness in the murky swamps of guilt — the vision of hope in the bleakness of desolation and despair — the vision of life in the valley of the shadow of death.

This is why the early church saw the crucifixion and the resurrection as one single redemptive event. The cross, without the resurrection, is a battle fought and lost. The resurrection, without the cross, is a meaningless victory without a battle fought. But, the crucifixion, plus the resurrection, is *the* redemptive act of God that turns the tides of history from the direction of ultimate defeat and death to the direction of eternal victory and everlasting life.

Lent is a time to remember what God has done, is doing, and will do for us. Lent is a time to remember what our lives would be if our Lord had not lived and died for us. Our Lenten stance is that of a group of people standing on the shore at the dawning of a new day. Looking toward the sea, they watch the flames of a burning ship in the bay. By a miraculous act of salvation they have been rescued from that sinking ship of flames. They are safe on the shore. They are delivered from a fiery death. The burning ship reflected on their faces constantly reminds them of the fate that would have been theirs had they not been rescued. As they look toward the sea beyond the burning ship, the first rays of the rising sun race across the horizon. They witness the beginning of a new day.

So, we stand at the entrance of Lent. In our vision is the burning ship of flames sinking into the sea and behind it the brilliant light of the rising sun. Both share our attention. The burning ship is the symbol of Joel's devastated fields left by the plague of locusts. At the same time, the burning ship is the symbol of the cross — the destructive death which would have been our final fate if it had not been for Christ our Lord. The rising sun is the symbol of the promise of the prophet Joel — the message of God's renewal and restoration. The rising sun is also the symbol of the resurrection which assures us of the new life we have forever in Christ. All of these visions, these images, these realities blend together to present to us the theme of Lent — devastation and renewal — perplexity and promise — crucifixion and resurrection — defeat and victory — death and life — a burning ship and a rising sun. All of these are one event in the mysterious and marvelous redemptive activities of God.

Lent is not a time to regret our faults or to rehearse our failures as much as it is a time to renew our faith that God is at work creating a promising future out of the mess that we have made of his world and of our lives.

Lent is not a time when we are to practice shallow fasting — giving up things we can easily do without. Lent is not a time to fast as it is a time to *fasten* our faith more tightly to the hope-filled promises of God.

Lent is a time to stand with the prophet Joel in the wastelands, left by the locusts, and to see ripe grain filling the fields. Lent is a time to stand on the shore and look beyond the sinking ship of flames and see the rising sun. Lent is a time to stand before the cross and to see it as the coronation throne of Christ our king.

Lent is a time to turn to the Bible — a time to study God's word and commune with him in prayer. Lent is a time to lift up the cross — not as a pious whip to inflict self-punishment upon ourselves, or as a gavel of judgment to condemn the wrongdoings of others. Rather, Lent is a time for us to lift high the cross — lift it high enough to permit the first rays of Easter morn to reflect upon its surface so that the cross might become a beacon of light for all the hopeless, desolate, and despairing people of our world. Lent is a time of renewal and of the restoration of our faith in the redemptive activities of God in history.

Late one evening, a pastor was in the pulpit practicing his Lenten sermon. In the back of the darkened church sat his small son. The sight of his father talking so seriously to a church filled with empty pews struck the little boy as being very funny — he laughed. Hearing this laughter, the father went to his son and gently said, "Don't you know that we don't laugh in church during Lent?"

"Why?" asked the boy.

"Because lent is a time when we remember that Jesus died for us," responded the father.

"Is Jesus dead?" inquired the son.

"No," answered the father, "Jesus died, but he didn't stay dead. He rose from the grave and is living in you and me right now."

The little boy thought for a moment, and then he said, "I think — I think it must have been — the Jesus alive in me that made me laugh."

Because Jesus lives in us, we face Lent with joy in our hearts. Not the hilarious kind of joy where we shout out "Hallelujah!" — not even the spontaneous and innocent joy expressed in the laughter of a little child — rather, the joy of Lent is the quiet, mature joy that comes from meditation and contemplation of what God has done for us. This kind of joy will open up our callous hearts and prepare us to really appreciate that morning — like no other morning — when a tomb stood empty in a garden and our Lord was released to conquer all powers and to exercise all authorities as he inhabits our world and us. Forever!

14

Names, Not Numbers

What comes to your mind when you hear the name "Moses"? Do you think of Charlton Heston standing on a rock with his hair and his beard and his robe blowing in the wind, while at the same time, beneath his feet the Red Sea churns and rolls back as mighty walls of waves forming a path for the fleeing Israelites? Perhaps you imagine Moses as a white-haired man standing on the jagged cliffs of a mountain and holding in his sinewy arms the two stone tablets of the law.

It is doubtful that any of you imagine Moses as a preacher; nevertheless, that is the picture of Moses which is presented in our First Lesson for today. The text is from the Book of Deuteronomy, which many early scholars considered to be a sermon spoken by Moses to the people of Israel. Deuteronomy has thirty-four chapters with each averaging 500 words. Taking into consideration the fact that the average person speaks 120 words a minute, this would mean that the sermon Moses preached lasted about three hours. That makes the Book of Deuteronomy one of the longest sermons in recorded history. However, more recent scholars have said that the Book of Deuteronomy is a collection of three sermons — which would cut the length of each down to one hour. Still, that would be lengthy by our standards today.

Our text for today comes from the second sermon in that series. The Israelites are poised in anticipation of crossing the Jordan River in hopes of taking possession of the Promised

Land. As they stand on this threshold of a new life with all its opportunities and dangers, the message of this particular sermon is "Remember." Moses exhorts the people to remember the gracious acts of God. Particularly, he insists that they never forget the exodus from Egypt. Also, he admonishes the people to remember the forty years spent in the wilderness. He urges the people to hold firm to their covenant with God, when they are confronted by the pagan religious practices, which he knows to be prevalent in the land of Canaan.

This is an emotionally-charged sermon in that God has forbidden Moses to enter the Promised Land with his people. Like a pastor preaching his or her farewell sermon to a congregation, Moses appeals to his people to remember all that he has said to them in the past.

The theme of the message of Moses is "Remember;" but more, "Remember who you are." They are the children of a loving Father God. They began as "nobody;" now, they are transformed into "somebody." The father of their heritage was a "wandering Aramean" — a nobody — a refugee without a homeland — a pilgrim who wandered on the wilderness road. They entered into Egypt with nothing. They lived in Egypt as slaves. Now, they are about tò possess a rich new land, to build a great nation, and to establish a royal lineage of mighty kings. Why? Is it because they are wise, or strong and brave, or faithful? No. Rather, it was because God had claimed them and had called them. He had chosen them to be his people — his beloved children.

This is the focal point of our text, and it is also the focal point of the Book of Deuteronomy. In fact, it is the focal point of the whole of both the Old and the New Testament as well. We are loved by God. Unworthy, as the Israelites were unworthy, God still loves and gives himself to us. We are his chosen children. We have value because of who we are; but more, we have value because of *whose* we are. We are the children of God.

This was important to Israel. Again and again, Israel had

survived destruction and persecution. As a people, they had known defeat and desolation. In every instance or situation, when all seemed lost, the Israelites remembered by whom and to whom they were chosen. They were "somebody." Their lives had significance, stability, and stamina because they were the called, the chosen, the children of God.

The fathers of modern psychology, Freud, Adler, and Jung, are recognized students of human nature. Their combined message to us is that to be truly human we need three things — significance, security, and love. For Israel, *and* for us, the ultimate source of our significance and security is to be realized in the covenant of God's love for us.

The tragedy is that Israel, and we as Christians, forget who we are and to whom we belong. We are tempted by our contemporary culture to turn away from the true God — only to worship false gods who demean our significance, offer little security, and show no love.

Lent calls us to renew our lives by remembering who we are and whose we are. For without this constant reminder, we are so easily tempted to follow every new fad that promises us significance, security, and love.

Today, the hunger for significance, security, and love tempt us to become status seekers. We think we can attain status by our conquest and control of material things. We are what we possess. The more riches of this world that we can grab hold of and claim for ourselves, the better will be our status in society.

We watch the TV program *Life Styles of the Rich and Famous*. Our idea of heaven becomes a Park Avenue apartment and a house on the Riviera with a yacht anchored in the harbor. Our Bible becomes the *Wall Street Journal*. Our church is a health spa where we go, not to save our souls, but to beautify our bodies. Our creed is the unholy trinity of competition, ambition, and social clout.

The real tragedy is that, in a status-seeking world of commercialism, we are important only because we are consumers.

We are not persons; we are purchasers. When we can no longer purchase, we perish.

A woman once asked her friends, "Why do you live in this broken-down neighborhood, when I know you have the means to live in a better one?" The friends answered in chorus, "You've heard of keeping up with the Joneses haven't you? Well, in this neighborhood, we *are* the Joneses."

Most of us desire to be the Joneses — to drive the most expensive cars — to live in the biggest house on the block — to dress in the most fashionable fad — to have a second house on the lake, or at the ocean, or in the mountains.

However, such a search for status is a poor substitute for true significance, security, and love. For when we face the situation honestly, we know that having status does not mean that people admire and love us as much as they envy what we possess. What is even worse, the things we own begin to take over, and soon it is our possessions that own us. We become locked into a rat-race to keep inflating our material life style. Luxuries become necessities. Gadgets become our gods. We spend more than we make, and we buy more than we need. As Oscar Wilde said of us, "Americans know the price of everything and the value of nothing."

The effort to achieve and to maintain status is ultimately self-defeating. It leads only to a lack of identity. We do not know who we are. All we know is what we earn and how much we possess. The Internal Revenue Service becomes our contemporary Satan who threatens to stick his pointed tail into our budgets and bank accounts — and audits us, and in the end takes all the profits out of our lives.

When we falter and fail to pay our bills, we discover that the gods which we worship have about as much compassion as a computer. We are not persons; we are a series of holes punched in a card. One smart fellow asked a computer if there was a God. The computer's answer came back, "There is *now!*" In a computer age, we are not names on the rolls of God's *Book of Life*; we are numbers on Social Security cards registered in Washington, D.C.

When we are asked to identify ourselves at a store in a mall or at the supermarket, the cashiers do not ask us what our name is; they just mumble, "Let me see your driver's license, please." And the stinging insult, in most cases, is that the cashiers never even look at our pictures. They just automatically copy down the numbers from our driver's license and mark the check, "OK."

A census taker went up to a house and knocked on the door. A mother came to the door. "How many children do you have?" the man asked the woman. "Well," she answered, "there is Steven and Kevin, Mary and Lois." At this point the census taker interrupted her impatiently, "The number, not the names, please." "But," said the mother, "my children do not have numbers; they have names."

Our names, yours and mine, are what give us significance, our security, and reflect the fact that we are loved. When our parents held us in their arms as the words of the baptismal rite were spoken and the water touched our heads, God laid his claim on us. By sign, symbol, and sacrament God claimed us — each and every one of us as his child — his chosen child. At that moment in time, significance, security, and love were ours. We became a member of the family of the faithful — sealed and securely fastened by "bloodties" to God because of the death and the resurrection of his son, our savior.

Moses stood by the river Jordan and faced the Promised Land. He said to the freed slaves of Egypt, "Remember who you are, and whose you are. You are the children of the mighty God." And, so they were. They had been baptized by the parted waters of the Red Sea. They had been confirmed through a wilderness experience. God had called, and claimed, and chosen them to be his children. So, today we stand at the First Sunday in Lent, and both the Old and the New Testaments cry out to us, "Remember! Remember you are the called and the chosen children of God."

Two men were discussing their Christian faith. One of them

said to the other, "What exactly does the gospel mean to you?" The other man thought for a while. Then, as if ignoring the question, he called his dog, "Come here, Lucky." The dog came. "Bark." The dog barked. "Now sit." The dog sat. "Now, lie down." The dog obediently settled down on the floor beside his master.

The man turned to his friend, "Well, as you can see for yourself, this is a good old dog. He is faithful, obedient, and affectionate. I'm fond of this old dog. I guess you could say that I love Lucky as much as any person can love a pet. But, look out there in the kitchen. There is my baby girl Susan. She is just about a year old. She wakes me up at all hours of the night demanding attention. She is not obedient. She throws her food all over the floor — and me. She will smile at anyone who picks her up and cuddles her."

"Faithful, obedient Old Lucky I'm fond of. You might say that I love him — but not like I love Susan. I love Susan so deeply that I would give my life for her; because, she is an extension of myself. Susan is my *child* — in her is my reason for living, my hope, my ultimate happiness. She gives my life significance, security, and love."

As Christians, we are not like "Old Lucky" — faithful, obedient, and affectionate. Rather, we are like Susan. We are someone's child. We are not God's pet; we are God's child. He loves us so much that he was willing to die for us.

Lent is a time of renewal — the renewal of our significance and the renewal of our security. Lent is a time to remember who we are and whose we are. Lent is a time to remember that the ultimate value of our life is not the "cash" that we possess but the cross and the crucified Christ we confess. He suffered and died that our lives might possess not worldly status, but rather eternal significance. He gave his life that we might be secure from the demeaning slavery of death. He rose from the grave that God's love might live in us. Therefore, this Lenten season, remember and rejoice. Remember the reliable, redeeming love of God for us. Rejoice. This, and this alone, gives true significance and security to our lives.

A Covenant Sealed By a Sacrifice

Our First Lesson today contains a bizarre and even a weird story. It sounds like an eerie tale of the occult rather than an account from Holy Scripture. God asked Abraham to bring him a cow, a goat, a ram, a turtledove, and a young pigeon. Abraham obeyed. He brought the animals before the Lord and slaughtered them. He cut each animal in half and laid the pieces in two neat rows.

Vultures hovered and circled over the slain beasts. Abraham flung his arms in a wild frenzy driving the birds of prey away. Exhausted from his vigil, Abraham fell into a deep sleep. The sun slowly settled beneath the horizon and a dreadfully dense darkness covered the land. Then, out of nowhere, a smoking fire pot and a flaming torch floated from the darkness. For a moment these two objects lingered and vacillated; then, the smoking pot and the flaming torch leisurely, but deliberately, passed between and among the carcasses of the animals that covered the ground. Then, as suddenly as they had appeared, the smoking pot and the flaming torch disappeared as if swallowed up by a demon of the darkness.

Now, this spooky scenario, as baffling as it may be to us, was not so baffling to Abraham. Rather, he saw this curious ceremony as a familiar ritual of covenant-making — a common spiritual experience of the divine presence. The smoking fire pot and the flaming torch were symbols that God was personally present. God was passing between and among the sacrificial animals to seal a covenant between himself and Abraham.

Before Abraham had slain the animals, the Lord came to him and said, "Fear not, Abraham, I am your shield; your reward shall be very great." Then, God made a promise to him that, even though he and his wife, Sarah, had been childless all through their long married life, a son would be born to them. Abraham would become the father of a mighty nation, and through him all the nations on earth would be blessed.

All the stories we read from the beginning of the Bible — the Garden of Eden, the slaying of Abel by Cain, Noah and the flood, the Tower of Babel — all of these stories are but a prologue to the profound moment when God confronted Abraham and called him to leave his native country for a new homeland: and, with the call came the promise: "I will make you a great nation and I will bless you . . . and by you all the families of the earth will be blessed." This divine promise of blessing runs like a golden thread through the woven tapestry of myth and legend, poetry and history which form the content of the Old and the New Testaments.

The God who had fashioned the heavens and the earth now narrows his creative concern until it concentrates upon the solitary figure of Abraham, the father of the people whom Yahweh chose for a special task in his overall plan for history. Coming almost immediately after the tragic story of the Tower of Babel, Abraham's call is like a burst of light that illumines the whole landscape of the biblical story. In contrast to the ambitious builders at Babel who aspired to make a name for themselves, God promises that he will make Abraham's name great. The people of Babel attempted to penetrate heaven and to touch God; Abraham knelt down in obedience and was touched by God. Abraham's greatness was not in himself, but in the God who had called and chosen him.

It is important for us to note that here we are not only dealing with a biography of a man named Abraham; he is more than an individual. Abraham is a personification of all the people whom God calls and chooses to be his children. As God established a covenant of promised blessings with Abraham, God also establishes a covenant with us. Abraham is truly our father-in-the-faith. We are heirs of Abraham; and, as heirs, we share with him God's promise that we will be his people and he will be our God. We are joined together with God in one inseparable union — one family bonded together in love. God, and God alone, seals this covenant-promise with a sacrifice.

The word "sacrifice" has negative overtones for most of us. Oh, we speak about the sacrifice of Christ on the cross, particularly, in this Lenten Season. We stress in our stewardship drives that we should sacrifice our time, our talents, and our income for the church, for missions, and for social services. We sacrifice for our children. We feed them, clothe them, and send them to college. Most of our experience with sacrifice is associated with suffering and the giving up of something that we cherish and desire for ourselves. Sacrifice is conceived of as a loss incurred without an expected return. However, in the Bible, sacrifice is associated with a gift gladly given. It is an offering which creates a special communion and an indissolvable union with our God. In the Bible, sacrifice is a means of releasing life in order that a greater life may be given to us. The focus is not on the loss, but the focus is on what is gained by the act of sacrifice.

The offering of a sacrifice was never thought of as an act of presenting the dead carcass of an animal to God; rather, the act of sacrifice was the releasing of the animal's potent life and the offering of that life to God. This "life" was conceived to be resident in the blood. The fact that the animal died was incidental. The important thing was that "life was in the blood." What was offered to God was not dead flesh but the blood of the animal which was filled with life. The body of the animal died, but its life lived on in the blood. It was this living blood of life — this "life in the blood" — that was offered to the Lord.

Broadly speaking, there are four basic types of sacrifice in the Bible. First, there is *human* sacrifice. There is little direct evidence of this in Scripture. The story of Abraham's willingness to sacrifice his son, Isaac, to God is a familiar and classic example. However, it was well known that in Canaan, as well as throughout the ancient world, human sacrifice was a common practice. The intervention of God in the Abraham and Isaac story, where God provided a ram for the sacrifice instead of Abraham's son, ended human sacrifices in the common worship practices of the Hebrew religion.

Secondly, there is *animal* sacrifice. It played an essential role in the religion of Israel, and it dominated the worship of the temple. However, the pre-exilic prophets — Amos, Hosea, Isaiah, and Jeremiah — condemned these sacrifices, and they strongly declared that animal sacrifices, even offered with the best of intentions, are less acceptable to God than the offering of a pure heart and a holy life.

This brings us to the third type of sacrifice — the *bloodless* sacrifice of a pure and an obedient life lived for the Lord. Paul powerfully presented this type of sacrifice when he wrote to the Christians at Rome. He appealed to the people that they should present their bodies as "a living sacrifice holy and acceptable to God." This, for Paul, is the true act of spiritual worship.

The fourth type of sacrifice is unique to the Bible. It is the *divine* sacrifice. The whole process of sacrifice is radically reversed. Instead of the people offering sacrifices to God, it is God who offers the sacrifice of himself *to* his people and *for* his people. This is prophetically implied in our text for this morning. In the visable signs of the smoking fire pot and the flaming torch, God himself is present, and he passes between the pieces of the slain animals; thereby, he offers the sacrifice of his holy presence and, at the same time, he seals his covenant-promise of blessings and love to Abraham and to us.

The most significant sacrifice that God offers to us is on Calvary. It is so significant that it ends the mandatory rite of blood-sacrifice in the biblical history of the church. God becomes incarnate, and he willingly goes to the cross where he sheds his life-giving blood for us.

The role that sacrifices have played in the history of the Bible and, in particular, the essential element of biblical sacrifice — namely, "the life is in the blood," is essential for our understanding of the crucifixion of our Lord. Christ died. True. But, what is so often overlooked is the profoundly important fact that he shed *his blood* for us. His life was not *taken* from him on the cross: his life was released on the cross. His life was *released* from the limitation of his body that it might flow into our bodies; thereby, this makes us one with him and, at the same time, seals for us God's promise of life — an abundant life of blessings for us as his children.

Every time we come to the communion table, we drink the life-giving blood of our Lord. We participate in the greatest and the final blood-sacrifice of all biblical history — the sacrifice of God himself — for us! Rejoice, because the blood of God flowing within us gives us eternal life.

Our librarian at Southern Seminary has a precocious preschooler. He attended Sunday church school and listened intently as his teacher described in detail the death of Jesus. She told her students how the Roman soldiers drove nails into the wrists of Jesus and how his blood spilled out on the ground.

The next day Charlie was playing in the backyard, and he snagged his finger on a broken tree limb. Charlie watched in horror as the blood began to flow from his wound. Charlie panicked. He ran to his father, "Daddy, Daddy that tree tore a hole in me and all my blood is running out. I'm going to die like Jesus."

Dr. Fritz took his son's hand and carefully dressed the wound on the cut finger. Then, holding his son's hand in his, he said, "Charlie, many times in your life, things are going to hurt you and cut you. You might bleed, but you will not die. Because Jesus died for you, you will never have to fear death for you will always be alive in him."

How true. Because God seals his covenant of love with the death of his son, Jesus Christ, we may bleed; but, we will never have to fear death. In the Bible, death is understood as the act of being separated from God. For Abraham and for us God sealed his covenant-promise that he would never leave us or forsake us. On the cross, God shed his blood as the final sacrifice that assures us that nothing can separate us from his love. A covenant is sealed by a sacrifice. This seal can never be broken because it bears the indelible blood of God himself. It is the royal insignia of the cross, which testifies to the fact that we are one with God. The blood of Christ flows in our bodies and enlivens our lives with eternity. We may bleed, but we will never fear death. Rejoice! Death is dead.

The Power To Defy Evil

Every evening the six o'clock news reminds us of the crime, the corruption, and the catastrophies of the world in which we live. It was in such troubled times and in such hopeless circumstances that a young Hebrew mother placed her baby in a basket and set it afloat among the reeds of the river Nile. Even if the baby were to live, she could only see an intolerable existence for him as he would groan under the burden of hard labor and be driven to the point of daily exhaustion by the sting of the slavemaster's whip.

Little did she know that in her desperation to save her child, the hand of God was at work. God had a plan — a great master-plan of redemption — to save not only this child, but through him countless children yet unborn. Neither did the Egyptian princess, who found the boat-like cradle at the river's edge, realize that she held in her arms one of the world's future great religious heroes — one who would one day hold in his arms the will of God's law chiseled into a stone from Mount Sinai.

The youth of Moses also fails to testify to his future greatness. One day, when he saw an Egyptian overlord beating a Hebrew slave, the hot temper of Moses exploded, and he killed the taskmaster on the spot. Fearing certain death because of his rash actions, he fled. No mark of a courageous hero here!

In the country of Midian, he married a wealthy man's daughter, and he became a successful sheep farmer. He was so content and happy in this new land that he did not even think of his own people, who were groaning under their bondage in far-off Egypt. No indication of a fearless liberator here.

Then one day, while tending his flocks, a bush burst into flames, and God called to him, "Come, I will send you to the Pharaoh that you may bring forth my people." You would think that Moses would have been overcome with awe and would have been filled with enthusiasm to take up the cause of his people by leading them to freedom. But, not so. He was too comfortable in his present circumstances. So, he attempted to refuse the call by claiming that he lacked the personal qualifications for such a task. But, God cut beneath this self-deceptive modesty. "I will be with you," said the Lord.

Moses still sought to escape. He argued, "I am not eloquent . . . I am slow of speech and of tongue." God answered back, "I will be with your mouth and teach you what you should speak."

Moses was caught. Reluctantly, he left the security of his tranquil rural life and returned to Egypt. God fulfilled his promise and worked with Moses, making him into a remarkable leader. With God's help, Moses won the confidence of the Hebrew people and courageously entered into conflict with the Pharaoh. He uttered the famous words that were to become the battle cry of the Black Freedom Movement in our own age: "Let my people go!"

Egypt's king was not impressed. He saw this demand as a trumped-up excuse to gain another holiday for his troublesome slaves. He closed his ears to the pleas of an oppressed people, and he ignored Moses. Even when Moses brought plagues upon the land, the catastrophies only provoked more obstinate refusals from the mighty Pharaoh.

Moses played his trump card — the death of the firstborn. This struck home to the very heart of the Pharaoh by taking his beloved son from him. The king of Egypt relented and set the Hebrew people free.

God had a plan, and God would not be thwarted. Despite

a reluctant Moses, the absolute authority of a Pharaoh, and the cavalry of a first-rate world power, that plan was brought to pass.

The story of the Passover and the deliverance of God's people is the central hub and heart of the entire Old Testament. When we hear it once again, it is obvious that it is a story which is executed according to the mind and the plan of God. This presents us with the sticky question: "Were Moses and the Pharaoh mere figures on a divine chessboard of history where all things are predetermined by God?" If so, what then of human freedom?

Where there is no human freedom, all of our efforts are in vain. Without human freedom, faith is a mockery. At the same time, if we deny the fact that God is totally in control of things, we then question the omnipotence of God. Either he is God or he is not. If he is limited in his control of existence, he then may be a mighty God, but he is not "all-mighty." Therefore, we can hardly confess in our creed, "I believe in God, the Father almighty."

It is a no-win situation. Assert the almightiness of God, and you deny human freedom. Cling to the belief that we are free agents in an open-ended world, and we are left with a mighty God who is not "all-mighty."

When we turn to the Bible, we discover that any rational attempt to understand the almightiness of God is overcome by an acceptance of the distinction between God hidden and God revealed. For the people of God in the Bible, the God who revealed himself to be in control of the world was a hidden God. God comes to this world and works in this world, but he always masks himself. In an angelic vision, in a voice from a burning bush, and in a night visitor God speaks to his people; but, they are never permitted to look upon his person or to behold his face.

The God of both the Old and the New Testaments reveals himself to us only where, when, and how he wills to be known. He neither throws open the gates of heaven, nor does he invite us in for a guided tour which is narrated by a celestial Barbara Walters. He does not do an intellectual striptease, and he does not show us the "behind-the-camera" workings of his inner mind. He does not take us up to heaven at all. He comes down to earth.

Even when we humbly seek for answers and cry out for insights and understandings, he directs us to see him only where he desires to reveal himself. He directs us to a cattle crib in Bethlehem, to the river Jordan, to the hills of Galilee, to an upper room, and most decisively, God directs our attention to a cross and an open tomb. Ask no more. Seek no more. God is almighty. God is in control of all things, and nothing happens that is not according to his plan; but, for us, the details of that total plan of redemption is still God's sacred secret.

What, then, do we say about evil? What do we say about all the demonic things that fill the tragic drama of our daily lives? The bloated bellies of starving children, the countless graves of unknown soldiers, the newborn entering into this world blind and crippled, the mentally retarded, the innocent victims of violence and disease, the suffering, the torture, the greed, the trail of blood and the broken lives left by a sadistic killer, the plague of AIDS — what do we say about these things? Are they also the result of God's will?

To this perplexing problem of suffering and evil in our world there is no answer except in the hiddenness of God. There is no neat theological solution. But, before we turn away in disdain and disgust, be cognizant of the evidence of experience that theological solutions and rational answers to evil are of little comfort when we actually face tragedy, sorrow, and suffering. When the circumstances of life really deliver the knock-out blow, it is not answers that we need. We need strength!

When Moses asked God how he could possess the personal power to challenge the might of the Pharaoh of Egypt, God simply answered him, "I will be with you." This is not just an answer; it is an assertion — an assertion that the presence of God is our power. So it is that we are to affirm life and to believe, even in the face of all evil, that God is good. Despite the negative evidence, God is in control of all things. God is present and his presence is our power.

The real issue is not what we can say theologically *about* evil; rather, the real issue is what can we say *to* evil. The ultimate test is whether or not we can stand bloodied and bruised by our struggle with suffering and evil and still be able to cry out, "I believe!" This is not a solution to the problem of evil. It does not explain where evil came from, how it started, or where it gets the power that it possesses. But, it is an answer — not an answer *about* evil — rather an answer *to* evil. It is the answer that God gave to Moses. It is the answer of God's presence, and *his* presence is power. This is a defiant answer. This is a daring answer. This is the answer of him who hangs on the cross and of us who stand at the foot of it.

Here at the cross, for one brief moment in history, we catch a vision of the strange secret — the sacred mystery of the almightiness of God revealed in humiliation. Here evil and all the demonic forces, armed with the power of darkness, encounter almighty God, and God conquers. God is victorious. God wins out over all evil. He does so because he is almighty, and he is in control of all things.

This does not satisfy the intellectual or the rational thinker. This does not convert the agnostic or convince the skeptic. They call it madness, and the world calls it foolishness; but, for us, who are being saved, it is the power of salvation. This is God reconciling the whole world to himself.

The six o'clock news still blares forth its headlines of blood and tears. What can we say about all this evil? Nothing. But, *there is much that we can say to it.* We can point to the babe in a basket, floating hopelessly among the reeds of the Nile, and to a helpless baby born in the feed trough of a cow barn. We can point to a young boy at a carpenter's bench and to a rabbi teaching, healing, and blessing as he walks the dusty roads of Palestine. But, most of all, we can point to a stark hill outside the walls of Jerusalem where a young man hangs naked on a cross. His innocent body is stained with spit, tears, and blood. His flesh is torn open by a spear. His brow is pierced by thorns. Yet, faced with this horror — this greatest of all evil acts — we can cry out, "Thou art the King of Glory!" In the victorious light of the cross, the issue of human freedom fades into the shadows. The problem of evil is not answered or solved — it is *conquered*. Rejoice. God is with us. God made the promise of his presence to Moses. God fulfilled the promise of his presence for us on the cross. Rejoice. The presence of God among us is power!

The Secret of Survival

Most of us will agree with the familiar adage, "Be it ever so humble, there's no place like home." We all need a place where we can go to be secure, wanted, and loved.

When God promised to deliver the Israelites from their bondage in Egypt, he also promised them a new homeland — a plot of ground that they could call their own — a land — a good fair land flowing with milk and honey.

After the miracle of their deliverance from Egypt, God's chosen people wandered in the wilderness for forty years. Finally, weary and travel-worn, they arrived at the river Jordan. The Promised Land was in their sight, but a raging river prevented them from entering. Once more God intervened. As he rolled back the waters of the Red Sea for their escape from Egypt, he now rolled back the turbulent waters of the river Jordan. The God-chosen people entered into the God-promised land.

This historic crossing of the river Jordan has been romanticized in hymns and in funeral sermons. It has become an image for the experience of crossing over the river of death into the safe haven of heaven. In reality, for the Israelites, the Promised Land was no paradise. Rather than being a land flowing with milk and honey, Palestine was a bare and a poverty-stricken country. It was a country of contrasts. The land was scarred by deep gorges and desolate wilderness. In many places, colossal erupted masses of volcanic rock provided the only shade; and, sources of water were scarce. Here and there, an oasis or a plateau appeared where various forms of vegetation thrived. The Promised Land was certainly not the lush garden of Eden that we commonly associate with heaven.

Moreover, to imply that God gave to the Israelites the gift of the Promised Land, neatly gift-wrapped and topped with a silk bow, is far from the truth. The gift of the Promised Land was more like a crated child's toy that must be laboriously assembled — attaching piece A to side C — with a special tool — that does not come in the kit. When the Israelites arrived in Canaan, it was already occupied by warring rulers, fortified cities, and belligerent inhabitants. The Promised Land was not a Utopia to be enjoyed. It was a pagan country to be conquered. It was not a gift as much as it was a conquest. If the land was to be theirs, the Israelites would have to work and to fight for it. And, so they did.

It took many generations — probably two-hundred years of victories and defeats, successes, and setbacks — before the Promised Land could be fully occupied by the Israelites. And even when Israel had formed a nation in the Promised Land, it was still no paradise. Sandwiched in between major world powers, Israel continually had to fight to secure her rights to the land. Again and again, the Israelites were captured by their enemies, enslaved, and driven from their land. Again and again, Israel made an exodus from exile and returned to the homeland to rebuild the nation. The whole history of Israel is the story of persecution and enslavement, exile and exodus, defeat and deliverance. When Jerusalem finally fell before the mighty political and military power of Rome, the Jews were scattered into the four corners of the earth. Historically, the Jews can be characterized as "a pilgrim people wandering in the wilderness of the world."

Recently, the Jews have returned to their homeland. But modern Palestine is still no paradise. The Promised Land is still not very promising. Today, the land of the prophets is an armed fortress threatened by radical terrorists. Daily, the

Jews struggle to survive in the caldron of clashing countries that currently compose the Middle East.

Now, what is it that we can learn from the secret of Israel's ability to survive? Possible solutions to this secret are many, and they are varied. Our First Lesson today suggests several reasons for the survival of God's chosen people. We shall look at two. The first reason is that, even though the Jews suffered, they never surrendered their belief in the one, holy, and transcendent God. At times, they argued with God.

They challenged him with their complaints. They disobeyed him. They hardened their hearts against him, and they turned away from him. They even openly rebelled against him, and they cursed his blessings. They disobeyed God; but, they never really disbelieved in him. When their faith faltered, a prophet was raised up among them, and they were called back to God.

Israel's relationship to God was both vertical and horizontal. God was, for Israel, "the great holy other"; but, at the same time, God was active as the Lord of history, and Israel's story was God's story. God was a faithful God, and he always heard his people's cry for mercy. Through all adversity, the Israelites held firm to the belief that their God had the power to intervene into history and to save them — to save them from their enemies and to save them from themselves. Their belief was based on their cultural experience. That experience was marked by many marvels and miracles — mighty acts of God done for them.

That is why, when the Israelites crossed the river Jordan and first set foot on the Promised Land, they called the place Gilgal, which means, "rolled away." In our text, the Lord said to Joshua, "Today I have removed from you the disgrace of being slaves in Egypt." God had *rolled away* the disgrace of being enslaved. God had *rolled away* the waters of the Red Sea. God had *rolled away* the waters of the river Jordan. Just as for us Christians, God *rolled away* the stone from the door of the tomb, and he released his son — and us — from the slavery of death.

The Israelites believed in a dependable world order. They were the people of the law — the law which had been chisled indelibly into stone. But, at the same time, they were convinced that over all creation, over all laws, over all order — their God reigned as supreme Lord and Master. He was not just a God who revealed himself in history; he was Lord over all history. He could intervene at any time and alter the course of their lives. He could even change the direction in which history would move.

Did you ever stop to consider why it is that you can turn on a faucet in an upstairs bathroom and still have running water? Water appears to flow upward in our homes even though the law of gravity states that water will only flow down hill. If you go out of your house and search various locations in your community, somewhere you will find a hill, and on top of it will stand a huge water tank. Most communities boldly display the name of their towns on these storage tanks. The water in your plumbing defies the law of gravity and flows up hill because the water stored in the tank of your community is higher than your house. The law of gravity has not been broken; it has simply been engineered — altered to serve our needs.

The life-flow of power into the Israelites defied the limitations of their moral character. This transcendent power within them enabled them to defy the overwhelming odds of their enemies' armies. Their strength to survive flowed from their faith-relationship with a transcendent God — a God who was behind them and in front of them; but, most of all, above them. This vertical relationship to God gave them the courage to challenge the impossible odds arrayed against them, and it also enabled them to persevere until they had won.

The secret of Israel's survival is that their God was not a prisoner in his world. Their God was a living, transcendent God. Because he was the Lord over all other gods, he could use nature and history to serve his purpose for his people. The secret of Israel's survival was the strength that they received from God, together with their unswerving belief that their God could do the impossible.

How big is your God? Is he the Lord over all of history? Does he hold the whole world in his hand? Or, is your God so small that he is confined to the church? Is your God so small that he can be contained in the limitations of a creed — or the description of a doctrine? Is he so small that he can be compressed, like a flower, between the pages of the Bible?

Or, is your God big enough to stand in judgment over the politics of all nations? Is your God big enough to move you to fight poverty and privation? Is your God big enough to strengthen you to stand up against injustice and intolerance? Is your God big enough to empower you to serve and to sacrifice your time and your talents willingly for others?

Is your God the God of Gilgal — the God who can *roll away* the Red Seas of this world and set people free? Is your God big enough to *roll away* the waters of Jordan and to deliver believers into the Promised Land of eternal life? Is your God big enough to work miracles and to perform marvelous and mighty acts?

If your God is not that big, then, he is not the God of the Israelites — nor the God of Abraham, Isaac, Jacob, and Joshua. Either your God is Lord *of* all, or he is not Lord *at* all.

The second insight that our text gives to us concerning the secret of Israel's survival is that they not only believed in an almighty God who could do the impossible; they also constantly remembered and celebrated God's mighty acts in history. The people of Israel never forgot the impossible things that God had done for them. When it appeared that God was doing nothing, the people of Israel remembered and celebrated the events of their past — when God had done everything. To endure and to survive, Israel stood steadfast in the present while celebrating the past.

Our Lesson today states that one of the first things that the Israelites did when they arrived in the Promised Land was to celebrate the Passover — the liturgical feast of their deliverance by God. Think of it! They were invading a foreign country with the wilderness behind them — the threat of hostile enemies all about them — the great battle of Jericho and a seemingly endless series of wars ahead of them — not knowing where their next meal was coming from. In such a critical crisis situation, the Israelites paused, took the time to worship, to celebrate the Passover, to pray and to praise God for what he had done for them in the past.

One Hebrew scholar has said that the Jews have been able to survive the darkness of the present because they live each day by the light of their past and in the light of their future. For the Jew, the past, the present, and the future are all one in God.

A little girl went on vacation with her parents to see the mountains for the first time. When they were driving in the mountains, their car entered the first tunnel of their trip. The little girl was frightened by the sudden darkness. Her mother leaned over and said to her, "Look. Look back at the entrance. See that light? Well, that same light is at the other end of the tunnel."

Later that day when the mother asked her daughter what had impressed her most about that first day in the mountains, the little girl answered, "I learned not to be afraid of the darkness in the tunnels because there is light at both ends."

What sustained the Israelites was that every time their history entered the darkness of a tunnel, they knew there was light at the other end. In every serious situation of persecution, enslavement, and suffering the Jews were able to sing and to dance before the altar of the Lord because their Lord was the Lord of light; and, he had created light at both ends of every tunnel.

Many times our lives enter into tunnels of darkness. It may be the tunnel of boredom, when life is dull and has no meaning. It may be a tunnel of disappointment, distress, and depression, when life seems hardly worth the effort. It may be a tunnel of sickness and terminal illness, when we feel hopeless and helpless. It may be a tunnel of family or financial problems that never end. It may be a tunnel of loneliness and death that seems to *be* the end. However, in all these trouble-tunnels of darkness, the witness of historic Israel to us is that there is light at both ends of the tunnel.

God is the God of the past, the present, and the future. Trust in him. Have faith in him. He is the Lord of light. In every moment of darkness, no matter how long the tunnel may be, God is with us. He can and will console and comfort us. He will sustain and strengthen us. Our God will rescue and redeem us.

When Christ was born, the light of a single star shone in the heavens. Saint John, in his gospel, proclaims to us that the darkness has never been able to put out that light. When Christ suffered and died, all creation moved into a tunnel of darkness. On Easter, the morning light of God flooded the tomb. Christ made a tunnel of the tomb, and for us that tunnel possesses no fears — there is light at both ends of the tunnel. Rejoice in that light. Rejoice in it and survive!

Praise God For Adversity

Praise fills the pages of the Bible and dominates our hymnals; but, it is often difficult to find it in us as Christians. Praise is not easy to define. Most Bible dictionaries include it under the general classification of prayer, and it is frequently associated with the act of thanksgiving.

In our First Lesson today, the author of Second Isaiah presents praise as the only response that a faithful people can make; because there is nothing else that God requires or desires.

God is about to do a great deed. It is deed before which all that God has done in the past fades into the background of redemptive history. Even the exodus from Egypt, so sacred in the memory of Israel's salvation, will be forgotten in the light of this new and mighty act. A new pathway through the waters of a new sea, a new way in the wilderness, a new river in the desert — all this God is about to accomplish in the process of fulfilling his promise to the people he has created and chosen. A new rescue, a new act of liberation, a new demonstration of God's continuing care for his people is about to surprise and to startle the whole of creation. Even the wild beasts and jackals and ostriches will bow down and give praise to the Lord.

This message from Isaiah is appropriate as we observe the last Sunday in Lent, and as we prepare to enter, through Palm Sunday, into the solemnities of Holy Week. Get ready to cut the palm branches from the trees, shed your coats, and fling them on the royal road to Jerusalem. Join the crowd of Passover-pilgrims. Shout with them their hallelujahs of praise to the Lord. God is coming: God is coming to turn history upside down, inside out, and right side up.

In our Second Lesson Paul writes, "Forgetting what lies behind and straining forward to what lies ahead, I press on toward the goal for the prize of the upward call of God in Christ Jesus."

The Gospel for today, despite its bloody parable of rejection, violence, and murder, rises to the heights of the holy promise as it proclaims, "The very stone which the builders rejected has become the head of the corner."

This Fifth Sunday in Lent is not a time for repentance and penitence; it is a time for praise! God declares that all that he has done, is doing, and will do for his people is directed to but one end — Praise! As our lesson tells us, ". . . that they might declare my praise."

Praise is easy when we have been blessed. It is easy to sing a stately and exultant doxology when we are in a comfortable church, surrounded by an affluent and a friendly congregation. It is quite another thing to praise God when we find ourselves in a family where there is constant friction. It is not easy to praise God when we are numbered among the unemployed, or the divorced, or the physically crippled, or the mentally handicapped. It is not easy to praise God when our life is truncated by a terminal disease. It is not easy to praise God when we are old and alone — in a lonely rest home, forgotten by family and friends. It is not easy to praise God when our waking life is more like a nightmare than a dream. Yet, the Book of Isaiah, from which our text comes, is a delicately woven tapestry where lament and praise, adversity and blessing are mingled together into one harmonious pattern. The design is clear: we are to praise God, not only for our blessings, but for our adversities as well.

Our First Lesson, which calls upon us to praise God, was written in a time of disaster and adversity. The cities of Judah had been left desolate by their enemies. The holy temple had been reduced to ruins. The people were in Babylonian exile. The Jewish nation had been robbed, ravished, and nearly eradicated from the face of the then-known world. Despite the disappointment of losing their homeland, the Jews, in their captivity, did experience some social and economic opportunities. They actually prospered in this foreign land. However, a serious problem confronted them. As they prospered, their religious faith began to fade. Torn from its historic moorings, their faith was slowly being drowned in the sea of Babylonian culture. The country that imprisoned them possessed a thriving agriculture and teeming industries. Even the Temple of Jerusalem paled into insignificance before the marvelous temples of Babylon. The Jews were frustrated and plagued with doubts. Why were the pagans so prosperous? Could the pagan gods be better and more powerful than the God of Israel? Babylon basked in blessings while they — the chosen people of God — had only a long history of suffering to look back on, and only the continuing judgment of God to look forward to. But despite their doubts, there was deep within the Jewish people a longing to go home. Their heritage had an irrestible hold on them. Palestine was their native land; and, for better or worse, Yahweh was their God.

Into this situation came the prophet Second Isaiah. He was a prophet of comfort. He proclaimed that divine judgment had already taken place. Israel had received double punishment for all her sins. Now, a new day was dawning. Yahweh was coming to release Israel from her bondage and to restore the shattered foundations of her homeland. Though the past was bitter, the future would be sweet. God was working good out of evil.

Helen Keller testifies in her autobiography, ''I thank God for my handicaps, for through them I found myself, my work, and my God.'' So, the people of Israel, having been blind and deaf to their God in the time of their blessings, heard and saw God at work in their suffering and adversities. Charles A.

Beard, the historian, says that one of the profound lessons of history can be summarized in the proverb, "The bee fertilizes the flower it robs." Israel's history of judgment, punishment, exile, and suffering was the fertilization of a renewed faith which was to give birth and nourishment to a new experience with the Lord. So, the prophet cries out to the people in their adversity, "Praise the Lord." Actually, the prophet was directing the people to praise God for their adversity as well as for their blessings.

Today, as the people of God, we are to praise God not just for the good things in life, not just for what is beautiful, or what is noble, or what is pleasing to us; rather, we are also to praise God for the ugly things in life, the ignoble, and the displeasing. We are to praise God for our troubles and heartaches, our pain and our suffering, our disappointments and our difficulties.

Now this may sound strange — and it is. It is strange in our success-oriented, pleasure-seeking culture. Yet, not only do we hear it from Second Isaiah, we also hear it from Paul, who thanks God for his weaknesses, which include his puzzling "thorn in the flesh." In Ephesians, Paul writes, "Always and for everything giving thanks in the name of our Lord, Jesus Christ . . ."

John Wesley, in his *Notes On The New Testament,* writes, "He that always prays is ever giving praise, whether in ease or in pain, both for prosperity and for the greatest adversity. He blesses God for all things."

Why is it that these great persons of the faith praise God for adversity? It cannot be better answered than by quoting Paul as he writes to the Christians in Rome, "God works everything for good with those who love him . . ." (Romans 8:28)

Praising God for adversity may at first sound strange; but, when one thinks about it, it does make sense. What are the alternatives to praising God in times of adversity? We could be indifferent and simply ignore adversity; but, it would still be there to plague us. We could become angry and resent adversity; but, that would only produce ulcers and cause heart attacks. We could judge ourselves and others by saying, "You only got what you deserved;" but, that would only leave us bitter and burdened with guilt. We could complain, grumble and gripe about adversity; but, that would only make us even more unhappy. Or, we could blame God for adversity; but, that would only rob us of all hope and would separate us from the one and only source of transcendent help that we all need in order to endure adversity.

When we praise God for adversity, we place our adversity into the hands of a loving and caring God who alone has the power to transform evil into good. That does make sense. Experience confirms in us that this is the only answer to adversity that can and will work.

To praise God for adversity does not mean that we assume that God is the author of all evil, all suffering, and all disasters. God does not punish us with adversity. God is not a stern-faced tyrant reaping his revenge on his renegade rebels. God is a loving and a forgiving Father. He is a patient creator who is in the process of forming and fashioning a people of faith — a people who freely and willingly praise him. They will praise him not just for his good and mighty works; rather, they will praise him for himself and for himself alone. God is a good God, and all that he gives to us is intended to be a good gift.

It is we who make evil out of good. It is we who pervert love into lust, plenty into poverty, differences into intolerance, and progress into oppression. It is we who make society into a seething caldron of crime, corruption, and combating forces. It is we who take a paradise and turn it into a pigsty. It is we who rape and ravage the natural resources of our world and turn gardens into garbage dumps. It is we who are the causes of our own adversity.

However, even though God does not cause adversity to be given to us, we can give our adversities to God. We can place all of the problems that we have created for ourselves into the hands of a recreating, renewing, and redeeming God. This is why we praise God for adversity; because in so doing we present to God our adversities that he might transform them into good.

Do you recall the phrase that came out of World War II: "Praise the Lord and pass the ammunition?" Originally it meant that we were to have both the dedication of faith and the determination to fight. However, with a slight alteration, this familiar phrase could be used to express the reason why we are able to praise God in the midst of adversity. The reworded version would be "Praise the Lord and he will *provide* the ammunition." When we hand over our adversities to God, and when we praise him at the same time, he will give to us the ammunition that will enable us to face our troubles and to fight them until they are defeated. There is no problem too big for God. His arsenal of weapons is sufficient to defeat the Devil and to destroy hell.

Particularly are we aware of this in Lent. The cross on Calvary was an ugly and an evil object of demonic hate and devilish revenge. It was created by society to crucify criminals and to eradicate rebels. Its intention was not just to kill but also to torture. The Gospels tell us that Christ went willingly to the cross and died for us. He permitted his innocent body to be nailed to that cross of suffering. Nails of iron were driven into his warm flesh. Sharp thorns pierced his bowed head. A pointed spear tore open his unblemished body. His parched lips cried out for a drink. The shock of this sacrifice shook the very foundations of existence. Darkness covered the land as if all creation were hiding its face in shame. But, through the dark clouds of this desolate scene, God the Father reached down and touched the cross — the ultimate sign of our human sinfulness — and it became the eternal sign of our salvation.

We praise God for the cross. We praise God for the death of our Lord. We do this not because we possess a perverted fascination, or a morbid attachment to gore; we do it because we see the glory in the cross and the glory of God incarnate in the crucified Christ. We see beyond the blood-stained wood

— we see beyond the twisted, tortured body of a victim — to the *victor*. We see the crucifixion as God's supreme act of transformation, whereby he changes and redeems a fallen world and makes of it a risen kingdom. As we come to the end of Lent, we raise our voices in praise. We praise God not only for our blessings but for our adversities as well. We know that praise is the appropriate response to God for both pleasure and pain. All praise, under any conditions or circumstances, brings us into the presence of God, and in his holy presence all evil is transformed into good.

This strange and mysterious act of praising God in adversity, as well as in times of blessing, could be summarized in one memorable sentence: "If you are dismayed with a problem that never ends, be encouraged by a strength that never fails." God is the only strength for us that will never fail. God, and God alone, can give us the tools to accomplish any task. God, and God alone, can give us the stamina and the courage to endure any suffering. God, and God alone, can give us the light to find our way in the most dense and most dread-filled darkness. God, and God alone, can give us the key that will unlock any door — even the door to the Kingdom of Heaven — the door to a new life that will never end.

Therefore, in all times, and in all places, and under all circumstances, praise the Lord. *Praise the Lord!*

Isaiah 50:4-9a   *The Sunday of the Passion*
                                                          Palm Sunday

A Sword and a Sacrament

It is Passion Sunday. It is Palm Sunday. Which is it? According to our church calendar, it is both. At first, it may sound that these two Sundays just do not belong together. Passion Sunday has to do with the cries of the crucified one hanging on a rough and splintery cross. Palm Sunday has to do with joyous "Alleluias" and palm branches raised in a salute to a king and to his victory. Suffering and salutes seem out of harmony with each other. Are we to cry out in terror; or, are we to shout out for joy?

It is helpful to look at the facts concerning the so-called "Triumphant Entrance into Jerusalem." Jesus did not enter Jerusalem; he invaded it. The entrance into the Holy City was not a political plan of the disciples; it was our Lord's personal and deliberate decision. His invasion of Jerusalem was an enacted parable. It was a sermon dramatized.

It is often pointed out that Jesus did not enter the city in triumph like a conquering king. There was no armed escort. There were no chariots, no jeweled robes, no marching soldiers, no shining shields, no flashing helmets, or no glittering spears. Yet, in truth, Jesus did enter Jerusalem as a king — a *conquering* king. True, he entered on a humble beast of burden rather than a charging steed. His escorts were not armed soldiers. They were common, ordinary civilians; but, these people were pilgrims celebrating the Passover. They were the "people of God." They were armed with majestic memories, enthusiastic hope, and the dedicated conviction that they were the called and the chosen children of the one true God. The Word of God was on their lips. That Word on their lips and in their hearts was as sharp as a two-edged sword. They cried out in the sacred words of the psalmist, "Blessed is the King who comes in the name of the Lord." Pageantry and pomp are present. People applaud and wave their palm branches. But, the power of the scene is to be found in the words of the psalmist; because history testifies to the fact that in the final outcome of any conflict, it is the word that proves mightier than the sword. This is particularly true when that word is the Word of God.

The truth is that Jesus did enter Jerusalem as a king; however, his was not the popular concept of kingship. Our Lord tried to make this clear to Pilate, later that same week, when he said, "My kingdom is not of this world." Our Lord came to Jerusalem as an invader to do battle. He came to declare war on the enemies of God. He came to conquer perversity, prejudice, and pride. He came completely armed; his weapons were a criminal's cross, innocent suffering, and an undeserved death; but, most of all, he came with the weighty weapons of the Will and the Word of God.

Our Lord entered Jerusalem with a mighty meekness. Our First Lesson this morning speaks to this point. It describes a kingship of which a crown of *suffering* and palm branches of *praise* are not only brought together; they belong together. A cross of suffering and palm branches of praise and victory are revealed to be inseparable in God's harmonious plan for the redemption of the world.

The author of our lesson is a prophet and a poet whom biblical scholars have nicknamed "Second Isaiah." His prophecy is an exultant proclamation of the good news. The people, who dwell in a perpetual nightmare of darkness, learn that a new day is dawning which will fulfill all their dreams. Captives are told that deliverance and freedom are on the way. The brokenhearted will be comforted. Those who suffer are promised relief. Each poem written by Second Isaiah is filled with the excitement and the expectancy of glorious events which are about to come to be. The horror of hell is being conquered and the coming of the kingdom of heaven is being fulfilled.

Our lesson reveals two insights into the unique kingship of Christ and the unprecedented presence of the Kingdom of God on earth. First, it points out that suffering is a weapon — a sword by which God conquers.

Most of us think in negative terms when we hear the word "suffering." It is an end-result that we would rather avoid. We live lives of careless dissipation, lack of self-discipline, and long-term abuse of our bodies. We come to one end — suffering. We do something morally wrong. We sin. We are disobedient to God's will, and he punishes us by making us suffer. Sometimes, we suffer without an apparent cause or an obvious reason. We believe ourselves to be victims of a blind fate; and, we fear that God is dead — or at least indifferent.

Isaiah, on the other hand, does not view suffering as a negative end of life; rather, he views suffering as a means of accomplishing redemption. It is a weapon — a sword with which to fight evil and to conquer it. Isaiah cries out, "I gave my back to the smiters . . . I hid not my face from shame and being spit upon . . . the Lord God helps me; who will declare me guilty?"

It is interesting that even though we use the word "suffering" as a noun, it always carries a verb-like meaning. It may be used as the object or the subject of a sentence; but, it still remains in our experience a verb — an action-loaded word. One knows from experience that, even though confined to a bed, or even if only sitting motionless in a chair, when one suffers, one is still doing something. Suffering is an active means, not a static end.

For Isaiah, suffering was a sword to be used to fight the good fight of faith. God was coming to liberate his people and to inaugurate his kingdom — and, the chief weapon in his hand was the sword of suffering. It was not the punishment of God's judgment; rather, suffering was a sword that was used by God and given to us to smite the enemy, to win the victory, and to usher in a new kingdom.

Isaiah was so excited and elated by the events surrounding the birth of this new kingdom that his words changed from prose to poetry. His words literally sing as he declares that Israel's nobility lies in her task of suffering. Israel would be highly exalted through, with, and by suffering. This was the deepest mystery of her calling. This mystery is personified in the figure of the Suffering Servant who would tread a path through defeat to victory. The method and the strategy of the kingdom to come are extraordinary. A secret to the world, redemptive suffering is a secret weapon that God and his people will use to destroy an old world and to create a new one.

Suffering is a sword to wield to win a victory. Secondly, our text points out that suffering is a *sacrament* to secure the peace for us. Our text says, "The Lord God has given me the tongue of those who are taught, that I may know how to sustain with a word him that is weary."

When we hear the word "sacrament," we generally think of the two sacraments of the church — baptism and communion. The Bible, however, is not so limited. In Holy Scriptures the one means of grace, properly understood, is *The Word*. It may take different forms. It may operate under the mask of water, or bread, or wine. It may be a word spoken or read. It may be a hymn sung or a picture seen. However and whenever, God gives himself to us personally, there is a sacrament. The cross of suffering and the palm branches of victory are united in the sacramental action of the grace of God. Israel had known bad days and good days; but all days were God's days, because he was their God and they were his people.

For the poet-prophet, Isaiah, the coming of God's Kingdom was such a magnificent event that no price was too high to pay, no experience was too repugnant to endure, and no method was too demanding to avoid. The end not only justified the means; it transformed the path of suffering into a glory road, a royal highway, and a via dolorosa!

The sheer enthusiasm and the complete conviction of the author of our text, that a victorious kingdom was coming, cannot be doubted. The profound and penetrating insight of Isaiah that suffering is not a negative end, but rather a positive means to an end, cannot be ignored. The fact that victory comes through defeat, and that salvation comes through suffering, cannot be denied. Suffering was and is a sacramental act of God's grace within us.

Scholars disagree as to whether the Suffering Servant of Isaiah is to be understood as a corporate or an individual figure. Most scholars agree that Second Isaiah was a great prophet; he had profound insight into how God was at work in the world. However, he was not a fortune-teller who was gazing into a crystal ball, seeing Jesus Christ being crucified on Calvary by the Romans. Isaiah was a man of vision, but his vision was that of a poet — the vision of words. As he spoke to Israel, he painted with his words a picture of the Suffering Servant; but, the title of his portrait was not "Jesus Christ of Nazareth." Its title was "True Israel." The Suffering Servant was what Israel, as a people down through history, had struggled to become but never could be; totally and completely faithful and obedient children of God. "True Israel" was a goal never achieved, a hope never realized, a dream never lived out in daily life — until!

Hundreds of years after Isaiah had lived, a baby was born in Bethlehem. He was an Israelite by birth. His human heritage was the history of Israel; but, his divine heritage was of God. This baby was more than an Israelite; he was the "True Israel." All of the history of God's dealings with his people had funneled down into this single life.

The poetic word-portrait of Isaiah's Suffering Servant took on flesh by becoming bone and marrow, muscle and meat. It was covered with skin under which flowed the body-blood of human life. However, Jesus Christ was not the incarnation of

Isaiah's Suffering Servant; rather, Jesus Christ was the incarnation of the *total* Word of God. He was what Isaiah could never have envisioned in the limitations of his humanness — Jesus the Christ, God become flesh!

We are grateful to Second Isaiah because his poetic vision enlightens our appreciation of the mighty and the unique act of God becoming flesh in Jesus Christ. Isaiah helps us to understand how suffering is both a sword and a sacrament. This does not eliminate suffering from our lives; but, it does give a positive insight to our experiences of suffering. It assures us that, no matter how great our suffering might be, it is not an end; but, it is a means. Suffering in the hand of God is a mighty sword that he can use to slay the enemy. Suffering is a sacrament — a means of grace through which God can give us more than victory. He can give us his holy peace, and a joy that passes all understanding.

Look at the palm branches in our church today. They are so delicate that they can be moved by the slightest breeze or the effortless wave of the hand; but, palm branches which are waved in conjunction with the Word of God become a sacrament in and through which God himself is present and active — dynamically active to establish his rule over all existence.

Look at the cross. Empty and unoccupied, it is simply an object of brass or the timbers of a tree; but, when the crucified and suffering body of Jesus Christ is placed on the historic cross of Calvary, it becomes a sword — a sword in the hand of God that can conquer everything in heaven and on earth. It can even destroy the very gates of hell. Alleluia! Rejoice! Blessed is the King who comes in the name of the Lord!

A Holy Hunger

Tonight we come to the altar-table to celebrate Holy Communion. Why do we say, "Holy Communion"? Is there such a thing as "unholy communion"? Yes, there is. When one comes to the Lord's table with a hardened heart and with a life that is turned in upon itself; when one comes with a proud and an arrogant attitude; and when one comes thinking that he or she is worthy of what is about to be received; then, that person will receive communion, but it will not be holy.

Jeremiah, who speaks to us in our First Lesson this evening, knew firsthand the difference between holy and unholy communion with God. His total prophecy is dominated by a tormenting tension between a covenant made by a faithful and holy God, versus a covenant broken by an unfaithful and a disobedient people. They had broken the covenant at its most vital point — at its heart. They were worshiping a plurality of gods instead of the one true God. They were baking cakes for Ishtar, Queen of Heaven — the pagan mother-goddess who was worshiped by the Assyrians and the Babylonians. They were practicing the barbarious rite of child sacrifice. Pagan abominations desecrated the temple. Worst of all, the people thought that they were getting away with worshiping many gods as long as they fumbled through the formalities of the ritual and the sacrifices of the temple.

All of these betrayals of the covenant tore at Jeremiah's heart. He stood in the temple courtyard watching the people as they wandered thoughtlessly through the massive bronze gates of the temple. Suddenly, Jeremiah mounted the steps of the temple, and he began to preach. It was more than just a sermon. It was a sharp and a harsh summons. It was a prophetic condemnation. He shouted forth, "Amend your ways and your doings." His voice echoed and re-echoed throughout the halls of the temple. The people possessed no true hunger for righteousness. They desired no warm covenant communion with their God. The people chanted glib words about the temple being the "Holy Place of God." The truth was that they had made of the temple — as Jesus was to say many years later — "a den to harbor thieves and robbers." Even though the voice of Jeremiah penetrated every corner of the temple, his words failed to break open the sin-deafened ears of the people.

Jeremiah agonized, even wept, over the incurable spiritual sickness of the people. They were a people with "a stubborn and rebellious heart." They had broken the covenant with their God, not only by their outward actions; but, much more seriously, they had broken the covenant within their hearts. The abominations of idolatry practiced, not only in the temple, but also on every high hill and under every green tree, were only outward symptoms of a deadly disease of disobedience which festered like a malignant cancer in their hearts.

Through this painfully accurate diagnosis of the fatal illness of the chosen people of God, Jeremiah was led by God to discover the cure. When Jerusalem fell to its enemies, when the temple was destroyed, and when the people were captured and driven into exile, the words of Jeremiah turned from the prediction of wrath, judgment, and doom to a prophecy of promise, forgiveness, and grace.

God revealed to Jeremiah that the wrack and ruin that had fallen on Judah were only acts of preparation that would enable God to rebuild a new people on the ruins and to renew a holy relationship with his people. God's purpose was not merely revenge and punishment. His intent was not to destroy the people with a mighty flood, as he had done in the days of Noah. God's purpose and intent were to sweep clean the false foundations of an unholy faithlessness in order that he could build and plant anew.

God loved his people, and that love was so great that he could not let his people go. God's love, working by means of judgment and its resulting destruction, would create a new people, a new covenant, and a new kingdom. The vision of this new beginning is profoundly expressed in the prophecy of the new covenant which is presented in our text for today. Like the old covenant, it will rest alone on the divine initiative of God's authority; however, unlike the old covenant, the new covenant will be an *inner* covenant. It will not be chiseled into tablets of stone; it will be indelibly written on the hearts of the chosen people of God.

This prophecy of a new covenant is appropriate for us to hear this evening. Especially, it is appropriate as we gather to celebrate the birth-event of the sacrament of communion. In the reading of the Gospel, we hear once again the familiar words that our Lord spoke to his disciples and to us: "This cup which is poured out for you is the new covenant in my blood."

Even more important for an understanding of what we are about to do, when we come to the altar-table to partake of communion, is Jeremiah's prophetic insight that what makes communion with God holy is a "clean heart." Now, the word "clean," used here, does not mean morally spotless or ethically hygienic; rather, it means what is intended when we say that we have "swept something clean." It means "empty." It means that all the trash that has accumulated in our hearts has been eliminated, thrown out, disposed of, and swept away. A clean heart is an *empty* heart; and, like an empty stomach, it spontaneously cries out to be fed and filled. With a clean heart, the whole person hungers and thirsts for righteousness — a right relationship with the Lord and a holy communion with our God.

Those of you who cook know that there is nothing worse than, after having spent long hours preparing a meal, seeing people come to the table and fuss over the food. They push the results of your hard labor around on their plates to create the impression that they have eaten something, when in truth, they have eaten nothing.

The main reason that we do not eat is the simple and the obvious fact that we are not hungry. If "Junior" or "Sister" devours two candy bars, downs a milk shake, and finishes off a twelve ounce Pepsi before coming home to dinner, *of course* neither one of them is going to want to eat dinner! Even the most favorite food will not be enticing to a body that is already stuffed full of junk-food.

What makes Holy Communion "holy" is hunger. If we come to the Lord's table full of hatred, or greed, or jealousy, or envy, or just full of our own self-centered pride — if we come to the Lord's table after having served the false gods of material wealth and earthly power all week long; then, no amount of rightly performed ritual is going to make communion "holy." The hungry heart is what makes communion holy.

Hunger of the stomach or of the heart is not a matter of the will. Sometimes, we can entice people to want to eat by the way in which we prepare and serve food. All of us have experienced not being aware that we were hungry until we came to the table. After surveying all the appetizing dishes of food, or after inhaling the tantalizing aromas drifting from the kitchen, hunger becomes obvious. An elegant restaurant which is tastefully decorated, enhanced by candlelight and "singing violins" can contribute to our enjoyment of dining. However, all of this does not create hunger as an act of will; rather, it only makes us aware of our hunger by appealing to the senses.

God prepares a dinner for us — communion. The one basic requirement for this communion to be holy *for us* is hunger — not the hunger of the stomach, but the hunger of our total being — the hunger of our hearts. It may be the hunger for the assurance of forgiveness, or it may be a hunger for experiencing the presence of Christ, or it may be the hunger for fellowship with God and with each other. No matter what basic desire or need causes us to be hungry, the experience of true preparation to receive the Lord's Supper is an inner emptiness that cries out to be filled.

That is why the warnings of Jeremiah fell on deafened ears; the people of Judah were not hungry. They had stuffed their lives full with spiritual junk-food — narrow nationalism, the teaching of false prophets, the following after of pagan idols, shallow ritualism, and immoral self-indulgences.

That is why Judas left the table before the meal was over. He was not hungry for the words of the Lord. His mind and his heart were full of self-devised schemes to take the destiny of the Lord into his own hands and to change the world; therefore, he failed to be present when our Lord declared that God was establishing a new covenant — a new relationship with his people — that would change the direction of the present world and the outcome of the future world as well.

For Judas, two thousand years ago, the meal that he ate with his Lord was the last supper he was to eat this side of hell. Because, after his act of betrayal, when he realized the irrevocable mistake that he had made, Judas truly hungered for God's forgiveness. He was driven not to the cross of our Lord, but to an empty tree where he hanged himself, to be left forever hungry for the forgiving words of God.

This term "The Last Supper" as a designation for communion is interesting. It appears nowhere in Scripture. For Judas, it is appropriate. In a sense, it is appropriate for *all* the disciples because it was the last meal that they would share with Jesus while he was in the flesh. However, in a far more profound sense, that communion which we remember this night, when the disciples broke bread with their Lord, would better be entitled "The First Supper." It was, and it is, the first supper of the new covenant. God was establishing a new world, and he began it with a fellowship meal. Our Lord sat at the table with a lingering look of love as he picked up the cup that was before him. He blessed it. Then he handed it to his friends saying, "This cup which is poured out for you is the new covenant in my blood."

God was moving from an outward relationship with his people to a new inner relationship. The revelation of redemption was rotated to a new focal point. The God, who had become flesh and had entered into the world, was now about to become spirit and to enter into our very hearts.

In our Second Lesson, the author of Hebrews places the new covenant in the comprehensive context of the Holy Trinity when he writes, "The Holy Spirit also bears witness to us . . . I will make with them a new covenant . . . I will put my laws on their hearts and write them on their minds." The Father establishes a new covenant with us by the blood of his Son. The Holy Spirit dwells within us, creating a holy hunger in our hearts for a continual communion with our God.

Rejoice. A new and living relationship with our God is now possible. It is a new covenant of love. It is not a new "rule" embedded in the law. It is an inner obedience rather than an outward observance. It is an act of forgiveness, rather, than an act of judgment. It is a gift of life, rather, than the wages of sin. It is grace — pure undeserved grace!

Therefore, let us rejoice as we come to this table, eat this bread, and drink this wine. It is the body of the living Lord. It is the life-giving blood of a new covenant. It shall never be broken because it possesses the sin-crushing strength of the cross — the life-giving power of an open tomb — and the live-preserving presence of the Holy Spirit. The cross, the empty tomb, and the Holy Spirit will come together and focus on your inner being, like a laser light, and will create within you — "A Holy Hunger!"

A Baptism of Blood

We cannot go back to Calvary. The cross was an event in history. It happened, never to be repeated. It was a deed of God determined, dared, and done. Our emotions may run high when we hear the words of the familiar spiritual, "Were you there when they crucified my Lord?" But, there is only one honest answer. No! We were *not* there. We are *here*, with two thousand years separating us from the cross on which our Lord died. The cross is dated; but, it is not out-dated. What happened then affects us now. Why? Because we come here today, not to admire a cross, but to adore a crucified Lord. The cross has rotted. The Lord has risen. The original cross of Calvary has long since rotted away and is no more. The crucified one is risen, and he lives forevermore.

This is good. It is not the wooden cross of Calvary that saves us; rather, the Christ who hung on that cross and who still lives today is our salvation. Therefore, we rejoice. Even though we cannot confront the historic cross, we can encounter the living Lord.

The cross is not only an act and a fact of history; it is also a symbol. It is not only a deed done; it is a sign which incorporates the basic plot and theme of our redemption. The cross says to us two things. First, we are, by our very nature, sinners. Second, God is, by his very nature, a forgiving and a faithful savior. Any effort to deny either our sinfulness or God's saviorhood is fatal to our faith.

In our First Lesson, Isaiah caught a vision of the conflict between human sinfulness and divine grace. Isaiah was a great prophet. He was tall enough to stand high above the people of his era to catch a God's-eye view of what was happening in his times. The people, each one by having turned his or her own way, were like sheep that had gone astray. Judah was a diseased nation dancing a "dance of death." The people practiced greed and injustice. The rich robbed the poor. Their lives were marked and marred by sensual indulgences and perversities. With scathing denunciation, Isaiah lashed out at their hypocritical religiosity.

Yet, despite the perverseness of the people, Isaiah was thoroughly convinced that Judah was the nation that God had chosen to be the Messianic Nation — the nation through whom a great and a wonderful blessing would one day come from God to all the nations of the earth. That blessing would come in the form of a servant of God — a suffering servant.

As we read Isaiah, his description of the Messiah is so similar to what we know about Jesus Christ that it sounds as if Isaiah stood tall enough to pierce into the future and to catch a vision of Calvary with Jesus of Nazareth being crucified by the Roman soldiers. Scholars of the Scriptures present convincing evidence that Isaiah was neither that tall, nor was his vision that photographic. Therefore, the value of Isaiah is that he did, with amazing accuracy, present to us a prophetic portrait of what kind of a Messiah was needed to accomplish the salvation of a disobedient, an unfaithful, and a sinful people.

Today, when we are preparing to call a pastor or to hire a person for a position of skill and responsibility, we develop what we call a "job description." This written description contains an inventory of the desirable personality traits and a list of the tasks to be done. This is what Isaiah does for us. He does not point seven hundred years into the future to Jesus Christ of Nazareth, identifying him as the Messiah; rather, Isaiah presents in poetic prophecy a job description of the kind of person that the Messiah will be and what tasks he will have to accomplish. He will be a suffering-servant savior. He will be despised and rejected. He will be acquainted with grief. He will be wounded for our transgressions. He will be bruised for our iniquities. As a lamb, he will be slaughtered. Even though he was without sin, he will be counted as a sinner. Also, he will bear on his back the burden for the sins of the world.

This vision from Isaiah is the key to understanding the cross as the saving solution to the conflict of our deliberate sinfulness and God's determined desire to save and to redeem us. The cross is more than just a revelation of our sinfulness and of God's forgiving grace; the cross is the means by which a deed is done by God. God is at work on that cross changing us from sinners into his obedient children. The cross does not just *say* something; it *does* something. The cross does something *to* us as well as *for* us. The cross is an act of creation. We need more than to realize the truth that God loves us despite our unworthiness. We need an act that changes and transforms us. We need to be reborn — baptized into a new life.

The knowledge that we are sinners cannot by itself save, nor can it change us. We know that it is better for us mentally and physically to love than it is to hate. We know that anger serves no purpose except to cause our blood pressure to soar, which harms the heart, and ultimately endangers life itself. However, just as surely as someone insults us or betrays us, we can produce a long list of reasons as to why we should make an exception in this particular case of insult or betrayal; therefore, our reaction is to hate rather than to love. We know that it is more practical and more efficient to be kind than it is to be nasty and hot-tempered. But, when we have a splitting headache or we are in a bad mood, we do not think; we just act, snap back, find fault, lash out, curse, or even strike our assailant.

We know that it is better for our happiness to be honest than it is to be dishonest: "Better humble than proud." We know that hope is better than despair, faith better than fear, forgiveness better than resentment, and industry better than idleness. We know all this! Nevertheless, in a given moment, we act or react spontaneously without thinking, without reasoning, or without considering the consequences. After the damage is done, we can give all manner of excuses and logical rationalizations for what we have done. We can even, at times, convince others that we were not really ourselves. The truth is, however, in our disobedience to God's will, we are our true selves. That is the problem. It is not what we do that is wrong; it is what *we are*. It is us. *We* are wrong. We are, as Isaiah says in the First Lesson, "strayed sheep." We have left God's path to follow a path of our own choosing. We know exactly where we are in relationship to our God. We have deliberately strayed from God's way. We know that we are wrong. Salvation is not a matter of *knowing;* it is a matter of *growing* — becoming a new and a different person.

We are possessed, taken captive, and held fast by something deep within ourselves that is evil. There is no amount of moral plastic surgery or ethical cosmetics that can change what we are inside. Beauty, it is said, is only skin deep, but sin is not. Sin is at the very depth of our nature. Sin is what we are.

This is why we need more than the historic event of the cross to enlighten us and to remind us of how much God loves us. We need a crucified Lord who can truly bear the burden of our sins and give us a new and a redeemed inner self. We need God to die for us. We need God to baptize us with his own sacrificial blood. We need to be made new persons. This is what only God, and God alone, can do.

When Jesus turned his face like flint toward Jerusalem and told his disciples that he was to be mocked, scourged, condemned, and crucified, the disciples did not hear. In their minds, the holy city of Jerusalem was the place where Christ would be crowned king and where they would hold places of honor beside him. They even argued about who should be at his right hand and who should be at his left. As they argued, our Lord asked them, "Are you able to drink of the cup that I shall drink of and to be baptized with the baptism that I am to be baptized with?" And the dumbfounded disciples answered, "We are able."

Generally, we do not associate baptism with the cross. Oh, we hear the words of the baptismal service which declares that in our baptismal experience we die with Christ and are raised with him to a new life. But baptism is associated with babies — not death.

When we participate in the baptismal liturgy and see the water in the font, do we ever think of blood? It is doubtful that we do. Water is a refreshing element. It is clear and clean — not at all like blood. But, there is blood in the baptismal waters, and we need to see it.

When we use the expression "blood is thicker than water," we are saying that being related to a person by blood bonds us in a very special way to that person. That is why to-day/tonight, on this Good Friday, we need to see the blood in the baptismal waters. The cross was our Lord's baptism of blood. If our Lord had not suffered and shed his blood on the cross, then the water of our baptism would be just water that would wash only the outside of our bodies like a shower or a bath. But, because of the shed blood of Christ, our baptism cleanses our innermost being, and gives us new life. Because of Christ's shed blood on the cross, and because that shed blood is in the waters of baptism, we are related to Christ in a special way. We are a blood-bought and blood-baptized people. Our Lord's shed blood not only gives us a new life; it also gives us a new relationship to him and to one another.

A pastor stood in an intensive care unit of a hospital. His mother was dying. He spoke to her softly, "Mother, do you want communion?" There was a long, silent stare and then the pastor's mother answered, "I want to be baptized." The son knew that his mother had been baptized and that baptism is a one-and-for-all-times event. He also knew that this was no time to teach his mother a lesson in theology. Then it occurred to him that what his mother desired was a reaffirmation of her baptism. As she was leaving this life, she wanted to hear once again the reassuring words that in her baptism she had been given a life that does not end. What should he do? Then he saw that a tear had fallen on the back of his hand. He dipped his finger into his own tear, and he made with it the sign of the cross on his mother's forehead. She died smiling.

This is the meaning of Good Friday. This is the day when the whole human race was baptized with the tears of a suffering savior. This is the day when we were washed by the blood of the Lamb of God who was slain for our sins. Our Lord's tears and his blood, shed on the cross, seal for us the sacrament of Holy Baptism and consecrate the wine of Holy Communion.

There is no need for us to go back in time to stand at the cross on Calvary. Because of Christ's baptism of blood and tears, we are moving *forward* to an unending glory. Therefore, rejoice! We have been baptized with blood and with tears. Now we are able to live with God forever in glory.

An Easter-Life

What does Easter mean to you? In the secular world, it means fluffy bunnies, brightly colored eggs, hidden baskets, and lots of lush chocolate candy. If you are a child, there is nothing wrong with this. Easter is a happy day, and God loves to hear the laughter of little children; but, if you are an adult and this is all that Easter means to you, then there is something tragically missing in your faith-life.

Interestingly enough, the word "Easter" appears nowhere in the Bible. The word "Easter" was originally a pagan term. It was the name of a spring festival in honor of the goddess of light and spring whose name in Anglo-Saxon was *Eastre*. Sometime, about the Eighth Century, the name was transformed by the Anglo-Saxons to the Christian festival that was designated to celebrate the resurrection of Christ.

However, for you as a Christian, what does Easter mean? Or, perhaps, more appropriately stated, as a Christian what does the resurrection of Christ mean personally to you? Most of you would probably say, "The resurrection of Christ means that I and my loved ones will be resurrected with Christ," or "The resurrection means eternal life — everlasting life." The more theologically oriented among you might say, "The resurrection is God's vindication of Christ's victory on the cross over sin, death, and the Devil." Now, all of these are good answers. Easter means all of this — and more!

Saint Peter, in the First Lesson this morning, gives a very

unusual and different answer to the meaning of the resurrection of our Lord. The text of the First Lesson comes from the Book of Acts. It is really a sermon which was preached by Saint Peter in the house of Cornelius, a Roman centurion, who was a Gentile. The sermon is short but tightly packed. Peter proclaims who the Christ is, and what he did. Peter also proclaims the power of the Holy Spirit.

The introduction and the conclusion of this sermon are pure Gospel gems. In the introduction, Peter makes the point that "God shows no partiality." Now, this statement is not as shocking to us as it was to those who first heard Peter preach it. This is true because there was, in those early days of the church, a strong group who believed that in order to become a Christian, a person first had to become a Jew. They followed the laws of purity to the letter. They also considered the Gentiles, and even the food they ate, as unclean. So, typical of impetuous old Saint Peter, in his sermon, he hit the heresy head-on, and he hit it hard. "God," he said, "shows no partiality." Christ is the Lord of all — both Jew and Gentile. Every person is clean because that person has been washed by the blood of the cross. Christ rose from the dead to give life to everyone.

However, it is the conclusion of Peter's sermon that is so provocative for the expansion of our concept of the meaning of Easter. Peter says, "He (Christ) commands us to preach to the people, and to testify that it is he who was ordained by God to be the judge of the living and the dead." Literally, what Peter is saying is that the resurrection means that we are to bear witness — to proclaim Jesus as the living Christ. When Peter uses the word "preach" here, he does not have in mind the image of a pastor, perched like a boiled egg in an egg cup that we call a pulpit. No. What he means is that we, who hear the message of Christ the Lord and his resurrection, are not only given the gift of the new redeemed life — we are also given the task of responsible witnessing. We are called by the Gospel to go out into the work-a-day world, and we are to testify to

Christ as the Risen Lord.

When we take the statement "God shows no partiality" and the call to "preach Christ," the message of Saint Peter comes through loud and clear to us. The resurrection of Christ is to be proclaimed to all the people who are outside our church this morning and who have not heard the Gospel — the Gospel of Jesus Christ and his victory over death and his lordship over life. The people of the secular world, of the Easter Bunny and the colored eggs, are all included among those for whom Christ died and to whom Christ desires to give new life. The world needs to hear that it also is included. "God shows no partiality."

In the body of his sermon, Saint Peter points out that God raised Jesus from the dead and showed him openly, not to all people — but only to his chosen witnesses. Now, these witnesses of the living Christ are to preach and to testify to all the world that Jesus Christ is Lord. Today, we are witnesses of the living Lord. We possess a message of good news that cries out to be shared.

If we were to publish in the church bulletin this morning the names of those who had won a million dollar lottery, and in the coming week you saw one of these people at the supermarket, or at the mall, or at work, would you hesitate to tell them the good news? *Of course not!* You would not be able to keep your mouth shut. You would shout out, "Hey, did you hear that you've won a million dollars?" Now, this is not to say that eternal life is a lottery, but the Gospel *is* good news about winners. The theology of the Gospel is that all people are winners. "God shows no partiality." He gives the first prize of salvation and of eternal life to all people.

The implications of what Saint Peter is preaching to us this morning is that the best evidence of the resurrection of the living and the life-giving Lord is to be found in our daily witness to Jesus Christ. This says to us that the resurrection means that God, not only desires to give eternal life *to* us; God also desires to give the gift of eternal life *through* us! The Risen

Lord actually lives, is alive, and is present today in our witness and in our testimony of his Gospel. As the Word became incarnate in Jesus of Nazareth, so the Gospel becomes incarnate in our words of witness and testimony. In a very real sense, our lives can be a "fifth gospel." There are four Gospels according to Matthew, Mark, Luke, and John — and, there is a "fifth gospel" according to us! As we witness and testify to Christ, the Gospel becomes alive in us, and Christ lives through us.

This does not mean that the Gospel is dependent upon us; nor does it mean that the Gospel would be silent without our testimony. Rather, it means that God desires to use us as the means by which Christ is to live today. If we fail to serve God, rest assured that God will find other means of making that presence of the Living Lord a life-giving force in our world. This truly means that God has granted us the privilege of witnessing. He has honored us with this responsibility.

It is not easy to witness. It is not easy to preach Christ to an indifferent and an unconcerned world. Most of us are too self-conscious, too timid, and even to embarrassed to make a public witness. However, God does not ask us to witness with our own strength. He gives us help. If you would take your Bible and read what follows in the Book of Acts, after our First Lesson, you would discover that the very next verse states, "While Peter was speaking these words, the Holy Spirit fell on those who heard the word." This morning you have not only heard the message that you are to proclaim, you have also received the power of the Holy Spirit which enables you to pass that word on to others. God never asks us to do anything that he does not, at the same time, give us the power to achieve. The living Lord is alive in you. He will enlighten and enliven you to proclaim his Gospel to the world.

In the novel, *Green Street*, the story is told of a lady who spent most of her youth taking care of her father. She was in love with a sea captain. Again and again, when he asked her to marry him, she would have to refuse because of the responsibility she had looking after her father.

Then, one day the captain told her that he was about to change his home port. Therefore, he would be leaving, and that this was the last chance for them to be married. If she wanted to marry him, she had to let him know before his ship sailed the next day. All afternoon and early into the evening she struggled with this proposal. Her father was a wealthy man. He could be well cared for without her. He had lived his life; now, she was going to live hers. She sat down and wrote a note accepting the sea captain's proposal. She knew that her brother would pass the captain's house on the way to work; so, she asked him to deliver her letter accepting the marriage proposal.

The morning came. She dressed, packed, and waited. The hours passed slowly by. Still, she waited. She rushed up to the second floor and ran to the window. To her horror, she saw the captain's ship sailing out of the harbor.

For the rest of her life she lived a lonely and a bitter existence. Her father and her brother died. She closed up the house, and she lived in it as if it were a tomb. Then, one day, when she was gathering her brother's clothes to store them in the attic, she came across the coat that her brother had worn on that fateful night — the night that had ruined her life. There, in the pocket of the coat, was her love note — still undelivered.

Today, there are many people all around you — in this community, perhaps living on your street — living lonely, bitter lives — lives spent in tombs of despair and depression because they have never heard the love note of the Gospel that God loved them so much that he sent his only son to die for them, and that he raised his son from the grave that they might be raised from their tombs of loneliness, bitterness, despair, and doom. Do not keep God's love note in your pocket. With the help of God, deliver it.

On this Easter day there is nothing wrong with hunting colored eggs or with eating chocolate candy. There is nothing wrong about coming here to church this morning and celebrating the resurrection of our Lord with hymns, prayers, and listening, once again, to the Easter story of the empty tomb. However, if that is all there is — if our celebration ends when we leave church this morning — then, Easter will have come and gone without any lasting meaning for our lives. On the other hand, if the end of this worship service is the beginning of your service of witnessing in the world to the presence of the living Lord; then, this Easter Sunday will not only be the first day of a new week — it will be the first day of an exhilarating new Easter-life — a life of never-ending joy.

The Symphony of God

This sermon is not for heroes. It is for the hesitant and the timid. This sermon is not for the militant who march in demonstrations of protest. It is for the meek who are afraid to act out their faith in public. This sermon is not for the players on the field who "suitup" and carry the ball; it is for the spectators who sit in the stadium. This sermon is for those who are not leaders, and who never will be. This is a sermon for ordinary people. Particularly, it is for the ordinary people who, because they cannot do something outstanding for the Lord, do nothing.

We begin, where we are — the Second Sunday of Easter. Traditionally, this is known as "Low Sunday," when church attendance hits a yearly all-time low, and the pastor's energy level is on "empty" after the rigorous demands of Lent and Holy Week. In most of our minds, the big event is over. We have celebrated the open tomb, the resurrection, and the living Lord. What could possibly top that? Our text this morning does not try to top the drama of the resurrection; rather, it stresses that the drama of the resurrection is far from over. It has just begun.

The story of our text is similar, at many points, to the Easter story. There is an imprisonment, guards, an angel, an open door, and a miraculous escape. Peter and the other apostles have been preaching about the risen Christ. They are arrested and thrown into jail. Suddenly, an angel appears and leads them past the guards through an opened iron gate to freedom. Then the angel says to them, "Go stand in the temple and speak to the people all the words of this life."

When the Sanhedrin — the full assembly of the elders of Israel — heard that the apostles had broken out of jail and were preaching to the people in the temple, they were at first puzzled, and then they became furious. Immediately, the captain, with his officers, was sent to arrest them. "But," the high priest adds, "arrest them without violence." This was said because, not only were the elders of Israel furious, they were afraid. Our text points out that the captain and his officers did not use force because they "were afraid of being stoned by the people."

For the second time, Peter and the apostles were arrested and brought, again, before the council of the temple. The high priest pointed an accusing finger at them and shouted, "We strictly charged you not to teach in his name, yet here you have filled Jerusalem with your teaching!" Then, Peter stood defiantly before the Sanhedrin and uttered some of the greatest words recorded in the New Testament: "We must obey God, rather than men." This is a story of raw courage. At the same time, it is a drama of daring determination.

The star players in this drama are Saint Peter and the high priest. They stood as provocative antagonists in the cloisters of the temple. Gathered about Saint Peter were a few of the apostles. Surrounding the high priest were the influential leaders of the elders of Israel. These two groups stood face to face, eye to eye, and toe to toe. The high priest and his supporters were angry, jealous, and fearful. Saint Peter and his followers were daring, dedicated, and determined. There was no compromise proposed. There was no treaty of peace possible. It was a duel to the death.

Now, as we picture this scene in our minds, there is an important and a most decisive element missing. It is missing because we have failed to hear all that the author of Acts is telling us. He records the conflict, which the early church encount ered, as it embarked upon its mission of proclaiming Christ to the world. We hear the general outline of the history of the church; but, that is all. However, when we read this passage of Scripture carefully, we will notice that, again and again, the writer speaks about "the people." They are not presented as props, nor are they used as parts of the scenery to enhance the drama; rather, the people are the real focal point of the whole drama.

When Peter and the apostles are miraculously rescued from prison, the angel tells them why they have been released. The angel says to them, "Preach to the people." When the apostles preached in the temple, the Sanhedrin, the high priest, and the Sadducees were furious; and, at the same time, they were afraid. Why? Why were these religious leaders afraid? Were they afraid because the message that was being proclaimed in the name of God was contrary to their beliefs? Perhaps. However, the heart and the core of the Sanhedrin's response of fury and fear revolved around one focal point — the potential power of the people. The leaders of Israel couldn't have cared less about an ignorant fisherman telling his tales about a carpenter's son, one who claimed to be the Messiah and was found guilty of treason; thereby, ending up on a criminal's cross. The Sanhedrin *did* care, however, that Peter and the apostles were spreading the rumor that the crucified one had risen and was still alive. The high priest, in particular, cared to the point of deep personal concern, that the people in the streets, in the synagogues, and in the temple were listening to this "fish-tale" about a risen Lord. The people were not only listening to it; they were believing it. And, the greatest concern of all was that the number of those listening and believing was growing by leaps and bounds each day.

The key to understanding the power, which the early church possessed, is the presence of the Holy Spirit. He was present; however, not in the form of a Casper-like ghost, hovering above the heads of the apostles. The Holy Spirit was present within the apostles and within those who listened and believed.

The Holy Spirit was present in the people, and that gave them a power which threatened the very structure of society.

The history of the early church, recorded in the Acts of the Apostles, seems at first reading, to focus only on the heroes. At first, Peter is the center of attention; then, Paul and his missionary journeys take center stage. They are the giants of the Book of Acts. They are the ones who spearheaded the expansion of the Christian faith around the world. But our fascination with the giants of the faith must not blind us to the fact that the decisive element in the history of the church *was* and *is* the people — the Spirit-filled people — the unknown, the unnamed, the common, and the ordinary people who were filled with the Holy Spirit. Thus, possessed with the power of the Holy Spirit, they not only heard, but they believed — and they followed. The people are the heart that beats beneath the skin and within the body of the recorded history of the church. Ordinary people, like you and like me, who do not make history — but who are enlivened by the Holy Spirit — make the history of the church possible.

This sermon began by saying that it was not a sermon for heroes, or for the militant, or for the quarterbacks who carry the ball; rather, it is a word for the hesitant, the timid, and the spectators of life. It is a word to those of us who recognize that we do not have the courage, the talent, or the skills to assume leadership in the church and to do something spectacular for the Lord — which, more than likely, includes most of us here this morning. We are ordinary people who live ordinary lives. We go to work at the office, or at the factory, or at the mill, or at the store, or we stay at home and work. We clean house and cook meals. We raise our children. We try to live as decent and as useful lives as possible. However, we are not leaders. We are petrified to speak in public. We believe in Christ. We love God. But, when we pray, we pray in private. Just as soon as the spotlight of attention moves our way, we head for the nearest exit and find somewhere to hide. If this describes you; then our text this morning has a message especially for you. It says to you, "Do not hide. You are important. You are an essential element of all history. Even greater, you in particular, are an important part of the history of the church." The church has been built, not only with the mighty rocks of faith such as a Saint Peter or a Saint Paul; but, it has also been built with thousands of pebbles and millions of grains of sand — the spirit-filled ordinary, "little" people who form and make possible the mighty structures of the church. You are the people — you are the people of God, and when God fills you with his Holy Spirit, little people — ordinary people can do big things and can accomplish extraordinary tasks. Never say to yourself, "Because I cannot do something spectacular and outstanding for the Lord, I might as well do nothing." Do *something*. No matter how small or insignificant the deed, do it! You are the people of God. The whole revelation of God is *to* you the people, and *for* you the people.

You may think that your effort would be only a "drop in the bucket." However, place a bucket under a dripping faucet. In no time at all, it will be filled. Or, consider a tiny snowflake that is hardly noticed when it falls on the back of your hand. Multiply those snowflakes, and they can become a power-packed avalanche capable of burying an entire city. The multiplication of those snowflakes can form a tremendous storm that can paralyze a mighty metropolis, like New York City.

What potential power that we, the people, possess when the Holy Spirit works in us and through us! God knows this. This is why every story of the Bible is without question grounded on the call of God to his people and their response. God continually calls his people to be faithful, not just in great deeds of courage and daring, but in the little day-by-day acts of faithful living that, when added all together, can create a mighty movement of faith.

Our text says that the Sanhedrin and the high priest feared the people. They knew that a word spoken possesses no power in and by itself; but, a word spoken by God and heard by his people — a people who are filled with the Holy Spirit — can change the whole world. And it did!

Did you ever stop to think about what the difference is between a grand piano and a pile of junk? Take some wires and pegs, some white keys and some black keys. Then, take some wood and some metal. Throw all of this in a pile, and you have junk. However, if you have a piano builder with a set of plans, that person can take that pile of junk and arrange its pieces into a grand piano. Then, if you add a composer, who can write a composition of music; and finally, if you add a musician, who can play the piano, you can have a thrilling concert, instead of silently staring at a soundless pile of junk.

The Bible tells us about a master builder, one who formed and fashioned all that exists out of a cosmic pile of junk. That junk the Bible refers to as "nothingness" or "void." The Bible also tells us of a composer, Christ the Lord, who wrote the music of mercy with the ink of his own blood and brought the sounds of a sinful humanity into harmony with a loving and a forgiving God. The Bible also tells us about an artist-performer, the Holy Spirit, who can bring the composition of Christ and the created instruments of God to life. And, if you add to this metaphor, violins and horns, kettle drums, brass and reed instruments, you can have an entire orchestra that can produce a glorious symphony of sounds.

Do you sometimes think that your life is more like a silent pile of useless junk rather than it is like a symphony? If so, listen to the Word of God. It is a story of a creator, a composer, and a conductor. But more — it is the story of simple ordinary things like a string, or a peg, or a white key, or a black key that are all part of the grand plan for producing the symphony of God. If you are a part of the whole, you are important. Your life *does* have meaning and value, if you have a part to play in God's symphony.

Rejoice. You are the people of God. You are the people whom God loves because you are a part of his whole creation plan. You are the people for whom and through whom a kingdom symphony is being created by God. Listen. The conductor is tapping his baton. Get ready. God is about to use you to produce a symphony of glorious sounds that will not only fill the halls of heaven, but will also change the very rhythmic pattern of history and determine the dominant tempo and the tune of eternity.

Acts 9:1-20   *The Third Sunday of Easter*

God is About to Strike

A brilliant light flashes. It strikes like lightning. Paul is shocked by a charge from heaven, and he is knocked from his horse. A voice vibrates about Paul which holds his attention in a vice-like grip. Paul is converted. The persecutor becomes the preacher.

The surprising element of this event is the realization that the conversion of Paul was the conversion of a radically religious person. Paul was the best of believers. Paul was a master of morality. He lived out every letter of the law. He was a superior student of the Scriptures. He was a dedicated defender of the demands of the law. Yet — he was converted.

For most of us, this fact undermines the very foundation of our understanding of the concept of conversion. From the social point of view, we associate conversion with rogues, reprobates, prostitutes, and law breakers. From the intellectual point of view, we think that conversion is what happens to unbelievers, agnostics, skeptics, and cynics. From the missionary point of view, we think that conversion is concerned with pagans, heathens, and idol worshipers. Religious conversion, in general, is for the ungodly, the wicked, and — *sinners*. The character of Paul fits into none of these categories. Paul's conversion was the conversion of an enthusiastic believer who was already totally committed to God. Paul's single ambition in life was to be a dedicated and an obedient servant of God's holy Law. Yet — Paul was converted.

The explanation of this strange fact is that Paul's conversion was not a moral or ethical conversion; it was a theological conversion. It was a conversion from death under the Law to a birth of life in the Gospel. In order to more completely understand the theological dimensions of Paul's conversion, let us review the story of our text.

A man, whose Greek or Roman name was Paul and whose Jewish name was Saul, had dedicated his life to the persecution and the actual killing of Christians in an all-out effort to destroy the church. Paul was on his way to Damascus, one of the oldest cities an the world. His heart was motivated by malice, and his mind was dead-set on murder. Paul was convinced that he was commissioned by God to destroy all the fool-hearted followers of the "Mad Messiah" — that pretentious peasant — that son of a village carpenter — that common "nobody" — who had made the blasphemous claim that he was the Christ, the Son of the Living God.

Paul was just outside the gates of the city when, suddenly, a blinding light flashed like a bolt of lightning from heaven. It enveloped him with a glowing circle of light. It was noonday, but this light was brighter and more brilliant than the sun. Paul was instantly knocked from his horse, and he lay prostrate on the ground. Like thunder, after the lightning, a voice rumbled around him saying, "Saul, Saul, why are you persecuting me?" It was not an angry voice; it was the deep and resonant voice of profound and passionate concern. When the voice was silent, Paul broke the stillness with his guilt-induced question: "Who are you, Lord?" And the amazing answer came back, "I am Jesus whom you are persecuting."

It is significant that, when our Lord identified himself to Paul, he used his earthly and human name — "Jesus." It is as if our Lord wanted it to be perfectly clear to Paul, that the one who spoke to him was the baby born at Bethlehem, the boy-child of the carpenter of Nazareth, and the young man who had been rejected and crucified in Jerusalem. It was the Jesus of Galilee, who had been raised and exalted by Paul's

God, who was speaking to him now.

The tremendous truth and the stark reality of this experience, that engulfed Paul like a tidal wave, was that conversion event which would sweep away all of the lies which had marked and motivated his life. Jesus reprimanded and charged Paul with the full force of the Law. Paul was judged found guilty, and executed. For all intents and purposes, Paul was experiencing a spiritual death that very noonday on the road to Damascus.

It is often said that Paul was converted on the road to Damascus. Strictly speaking, this is not the whole truth. The truth is that his conversion-experience only had its beginning on the road to Damascus. The conversion of Paul, like all true conversions, came in the form of two acts. The first act was his experience of being struck dead by the Law. The second act was his being raised up to a new life by the Gospel. Paul had experienced the gavel of the law, as it hammered his haughtiness to a devastating death. Paul was personally experiencing what he would later proclaim in his preaching, "The law kills; the Spirit alone gives life."

In the first act, the sign of Paul's experience of death was his blindness. Our text states, ". . . when his eyes were opened, he could see nothing." So, the irony of ironies is that the proud and the boastful conqueror for God, who had set out for Damascus with a mission to kill Christians and to eradicate the church, was led into the city as a poor and blind beggar.

The second act of Paul's conversion occurred in Damascus. Having received the blinding death-blow of the Law, he was then prepared to receive the life-giving blessing of the Gospel. Ananias, directed by God, placed his hands upon Paul's head. He absolved him of all sins. He commanded him to no longer persecute Christians; rather, he commissioned Paul to preach the living Lord, Jesus the Christ. The Holy Spirit entered into Paul. The scales fell from his eyes. His sight was restored. He was baptized. He ate food with the disciples. Therefore, being fully nourished and strengthened by food and by the Spirit of Christ, Paul immediately went to the nearest synagogue, where he began to preach the crucified and risen Lord — the Son of the Holy God.

Paul was converted by the Law and by the Gospel. However one more act needs to be added to this drama of Paul's conversion, and one more step needs to be stressed. It is this final act that points out what Paul's conversion means to us today.

The third act, the final step of Paul's conversion, was *the conversion of the word, that he had heard, into the energetic life of faith, that he lived.* After, as well as before, his conversion, Paul was a student of the Word. It was the Word that was the driving force of his life. Paul was an energetic, an enthusiastic, and a dedicated "doer" of the Word. His conversion simply redirected his energies and transformed his enthusiasm from persecution to proclamation. The Word heard was a generator of energy that electrified his life and moved him into immediate action — both before and after his conversion.

Now this third act of Paul's conversion — the conversion of the Word that he heard into his energetic life, which he then lived — is the conversion that we do desperately need. We all need the conversion of our convictions into actions — dedication into deeds. We need to let the power of the Word, the word that we hear, radiate through us into the energetic lives of faith that we live. It is like harnessing the gravity pull of a great waterfall into electrical power in order to light our homes. It is like harnessing the sunlight as solar energy to heat our homes. The power is there; it only needs to be transformed. It needs to be converted from one form of power to another.

The tragedy of our lives is that, somewhere along the power-line, the energy of the Word gets short-circuited, and the conversion of energy never takes place. As transformers of the Word, we fail; and most likely, the fuse-blowing point of our failure is our pride. We are afraid of what others will think about us or what they will say about us if we become too enthusiastic about our faith. Nobody wants to be labeled a "do-gooder," or a "fanatic," or a "religious nut." We do not want to be labeled or laughed at. So, we play it cool. We adopt an air of sophistication. We become blase; this causes us never to get excited about anything. Far too often, we go through life anxiously looking in the rear-view mirror to see what others are thinking about us; thus, all the while, we stay in second gear and never shift into high. No danger here! Only dullness.

The power of the Word of God never converts into enthusiastic actions in our lives. Far too quickly, we short-circuit it into carefully worded, well-guarded, and conservative expressions of our faith. We never risk radical involvement or commitment. We avoid all overstatements and spontaneous expressions of emotion. We play it safe.

This tragic short-circuiting of the power of the Word of God prohibits us from ever being converted into energetic believers, and it robs us, not only of knowing the full joy of a dynamic faith, but also of experiencing a truly Christian style of life. For example, take forgiveness, and love, and service to others — actions which characterize the active will of God in our lives. Without enthusiasm, these actions never quite measure up to what the New Testament is talking about when it uses these words. Forgiveness, without enthusiasm, becomes a duty that is grudgingly done. Love becomes just another law to be obeyed. Service becomes a slavish demand, which we practice like a dull discipline — rather than it being a deed we are delighted to do.

Without enthusiasm, God's will becomes a series of tasks that we must do. We actually exhaust ourselves trying to do them. In reality, they are things that we *can* do joyfully, because we are plugged into a potential powerhouse of unlimited energy which constantly flows from the Word of God.

Before this sermon ends, let there be no conclusions drawn that this sermon is a "you should" or a "you must" kind of sermon which makes an appeal — even a demand — for you to "do something." The intention of this sermon is to place no demands upon you as a listener — whatsoever. The intent of this sermon is to confront you with a "you will" message. The theme of this sermon is not a demand; instead, it is a *declaration*. It is a promise from God that he will not rest until the current is restored to our lives and until his Word flows through us and moves us to expressive actions of faith.

In our text, Paul did not go to Damascus to be converted. Our text is not primarily about what Paul did; rather, it is about *what God did to Paul*. God is the aggressive actor in the drama of salvation. God writes, directs, produces, and stars in the drama of conversion. It was God who knocked Paul from his horse to the ground. It was God who blinded Paul with the judgmental word of the Law. It was God who restored Paul's sight with the gift of the Gospel. It was God who forgave, and blessed, and commissioned Paul. And, God is determined to do the same thing to you and to me. God will strike us, again and again, with his Word, until that Word makes contact and becomes active in our lives.

The Word of God is like lightning. It does not strike when we want it to. We cannot, by any power of our own will or self-determination, cause lightning to occur. Lightning strikes when the conditions are right. So it is with the Word of God. In God's good time, we will experience the striking surge of the power of his Word in our lives; and, we *will* express our faith in action.

Look up. The dark clouds are gathering. The wind is changing, and there is a refreshing scent in the air. The heavens are charged with power. Any moment now, there will be a bolt from the blue, and our lives will be radically changed. The Word of God that we hear will be electrified into new energies for the lives that we live.

Warning! God is about to strike!

Acts 13:15-16, 26-33   **The Fourth Sunday of Easter**

The Mystery of God's Mercy

Have you ever hurt someone, or have you ever insulted someone without knowing it? Have you ever offended a friend, or slighted a spouse? Of course you have. All of us have. And, when we find out what hurt or harm our actions have caused, we say, "I didn't understand. I didn't know." We are sorry. We regret it; but, it is too late. A revealing scar is left. It is like driving a nail into a piece of lumber. You make a mistake. That is not exactly where you wanted it. So, you take the claw-end of a hammer, and pull the nail out. The nail is gone; but the piece of wood is marred. A scar remains.

In our text this morning, Paul is preaching a sermon about some people who drove nails into two pieces of wood which formed a cross. On it they crucified the Son of God. Paul is preaching to the Jews. He addresses them as "Sons of Abraham." He tells that, when the people of Jerusalem encountered Jesus, the Messiah, in the flesh, they failed to recognize him. Even though they went to the synagogue every Sabbath and heard the reading of the prophets foretelling the coming of Christ, they did not understand. They did not know. They listened, but they did not hear. God revealed to them in the Holy Scriptures what he was going to do. He foretold the coming of the Savior. God even revealed how his chosen people would reject the Savior, deny him, and kill him. They listened but they did not hear. As Paul puts it in our text, ". . . they did not recognize him nor understand the utterances of the prophets. . ." Now, it is true that Jesus was not murdered; he was legally executed. It is also true that the Jews did not drive the nails into our Lord's wrists and feet; the Roman soldiers did. The people of Jerusalem could have legitimately "passed the buck" by saying, "We did not cause the death of Jesus; the leaders of our religion did it." In turn, the leaders of Israel could have avoided their responsibility for the crucifixion by saying, "We have no legal power to execute anyone by crucifixion." They would be right because they did not. Pilate is the one who sentenced Jesus to death.

However, the purpose of this sermon is not to lay a "guilt trip" on anyone. The truth is that the death of our Lord is so tangled up in such a web of legal and illegal maneuvers that the smartest group of criminal lawyers today would not be able to build an open-and-shut case that would convince an impartial jury who the culprit was that really had been responsible for the killing of Jesus. Pilate would not have done what he did without the request — accompanied by a subtle threat — from the Sanhedrin. And, the Jewish leaders could not have done what they did without the support and the consent of the people. And, the people did not know what they were doing. From the cross, Jesus himself, said to God concerning the people, ". . . they know not what they do."

The people did not know or understand what they were doing because their ears were deafened and their eyes were blinded by sin. The power of sin held the people in its vicelike grip. This is the same sin, we might add, that so often blinds our eyes of faith and deafens our ears to the Word of God. Whenever we hurt or harm someone, knowingly or because of ignorance, we participate in the activities of that universal demonic power. The Evil One holds us and our world as prisoners. Flip Wilson was right — seriously right — when he comically remarked, "The Devil made me do it." The root source is the Evil One, who sets in motion the events — then and now — that ultimately lead to the continuous denial, the betrayal, and the death of our Lord. Every evil deed we do drives another nail into the flesh of our Lord.

If anyone is guilty, all are guilty — because, all are sinners. This was the assumption undergirding all that Paul preached in his sermons and wrote in his letters. We are all guilty because all have sinned. But the final conclusion of Paul, in all that he says, is not the bad news of sin — but rather the good news of salvation. We are all saved because Christ died for us all.

In our text today, Paul not only points to the good news, he also says something else that is not as clear or as obvious as his sin-and-salvation motif. Paul says to the Jews that, in their ignorance and misunderstanding of the prophets, they fulfilled the will of God. Stop for a moment and consider what Paul is saying. He says that the Jews heard the prophets. The Jews did not understand what they heard. However, in their ignorance, they fulfilled the will of God.

What Paul is saying is that God told the people that they would kill the Messiah whom he would send. The people did not understand what God was telling them they would do; but, they did it anyway. They did, without even knowing it, exactly what God said they would do. They killed the Messiah.

What are we to make of this? Is Paul saying to us that we are a predestined people? Is he saying that God predetermines everything that we are going to do before we do it? In addition, is Paul saying that we still do not know what we have done, even after we have done it? Are memory and knowledge, understanding and belief meaningless? Are they meaningless because what we do is ultimately decided by God? Are we puppets instead of people reacting automatically to the pull of preset strings?

No. Paul is not saying this. When Paul says that even through ignorance of God's word, the Jews fulfilled the will of God, he is simply acknowledging the *limitations* of human knowledge and understanding. Paul is saying that so far as our salvation is concerned, human knowledge is ineffective and powerless. Our knowledge of the things of this world is apparently boundless. We can invent plastics, transplant human hearts, send satellites to distant planets, and plumb the depths of the sea; but we cannot, by our own knowledge or understanding, save ourselves. Human knowledge cannot frustrate God's plans. Human knowledge cannot crucify Christ nor can human knowledge raise him from the dead. God, and God alone, can. God alone decided that his son had to die and that he had to be raised from the dead. God determined it. God dared it. God did it.

This undoubtedly raises more questions in your minds than answers. The truth is that when we stand before the cross and the opened tomb, we stand before two of the greatest mysteries of history. The more we study, learn, and know about these mysteries, the more we know that we do not know. The deeper we delve into the depths of these mysteries, the more mysterious they become.

This is good news for two reasons. First, it says to us not only that we *cannot* know everything, but that we do not *need* to know everything in order to be saved. It is not the amount of our intelligence or the accuracy of our knowledge that saves us. God, and God alone, saves us. His knowledge of us — not our knowledge of him — is the basis of our salvation.

Paul and Luther both cry out to us from the depths of their spiritual struggle that we are justified by faith and not by our good works. Paul Tillich, a giant among theologians, speaking to the intellectuals of our age, states that we are justified by faith, not only apart from our good works, but also *apart from our knowledge and understanding of God* as well. For the majority of us, this is good news. This is good news because we are not pious saints of perfected piety, nor are we brilliant scholars or post-graduate theologians. We are weak and helpless mortals. We rejoice in the fact that we are saved by God's wisdom and knowledge — and by God's piety and purity. We rejoice that we are saved by grace and by grace alone.

Second, the mystery surrounding the process of our

salvation is good because, it helps us to accept the mystery of life — *all* of life. Ask any group of scientific scholars, "What is the most fascinating fact about life?" They will probably tell you the same thing, the more they know about their own field of expertise, the more they know that they do not know. Life is emotionally exciting and intellectually stimulating because the solving of one mystery only creates other mysteries yet to be solved. There is a secret pattern to all life. One thing is related to another, and everything is related to all other things. Everything has a purpose that fits into the overall pattern of existence.

Take nature for example. More particularly, take snakes (which are a part of nature). Snakes are perhaps the most universally hated and feared creatures in all of God's world. However, it you were to encounter a member of an organization in Miami, Florida, called "Reptile Rescuers," you would hear a far different story. Their business is to save snakes from being killed by panicky people. These reptile redeemers will talk for hours about the absolute and vital role that snakes play in the balance of nature.

Everything in nature and everything in life has a purpose. We may not know or understand that purpose, but it governs our lives. Everything in our lives and everything that happens to us has a purpose in God's plan for us and for our lives. We may not understand it. We may question God and even challenge him. We may even doubt him. Like the people of Jerusalem about whom Paul is talking in our text this morning, we may also go so far as to desire the very death of God. But, the truth remains that human knowledge and understanding are poor, at best, and are seriously limited in solving the basic meaning and purpose of life. The ultimate meaning of life is hidden in the mystery of God himself.

Despite the fact that God has revealed so much of himself to us, God still is God. The details of his will for us and for our world are a divine mystery. No amount of pious praying can probe the mystery of why God permits a particular disaster, tragedy, or experience of suffering to happen in our lives. No amount of brilliant biblical research can satisfyingly answer the question, "Why does God permit this to happen to me?" A baby is born blind. A teenager is helplessly hooked on Crack. A parent-provider for a family is struck down in middle age by cancer. A faithful saint of the church is confined to a nursing home and loses all human dignity while enduring a lingering death. No pulpit prince can ever preach a sermon that will justify these facts of life in the light of a compassionate and a loving God.

All we can know (and this only partially) is that everything that happens will eventually find a place in the ultimate plan of God. God does not grant us theological or biblical expertise. He only grants us the power and the spiritual strength to trust him — to trust that he is still in control. And, ultimately everything which happens has a positive purpose in his plan for us and for our eternal destiny. Everything — absolutely *everything* — is transformed into good by the mystery of the providential power of God. One day, when we do see God face to face, it will be a compassionate and a loving face that confronts us and comforts us. He will wipe away all our tears and eliminate all our questions, doubts, and fears by the mysterious presence of his holy love.

In the classic story, *The Monkey's Paw*, a friend gives to a poor man and his wife a petrified monkey's paw which has the magical power to grant three wishes. The first wish of these poor people is for wealth — five hundred pounds. There is a knock at the door, and a man from the town factory delivers the sad news that their son has fallen into the grinding machinery of the mill. He has been instantly killed. Then, the messenger presents them with a compensation check for five hundred pounds. They panic! They grab the monkey's paw. They wish their son to be alive again.

Another knock is heard at the door. They rush to open the door, and there stands their son. Yes, he is alive, but his body is torn and twisted in painful agony. They are horrified at the monsterous sight of their son and his pleading appeals for mercy. They grab the monkey's paw. With their third and last wish, they wish their son dead again — dead and at peace.

The universal and enduring popularity of this classic story, *The Monkey's Paw*, is that it speaks to a deep desire within all of us for the possession of magical wishes to get anything that we desire. Most of us really prefer magic rather than mystery. We want our prayers to work magic for us. We want God to be like a super slot-machine that, if we pull the right handle of faith, we will hit the giant jackpot, win the lottery of life, magically have all of our dreams come true immediately, and have all our desperate desires instantly granted.

God, however, is not a God of magical powers. He is a God of mysterious powers. He gives us no monkey's paw which possesses three magic wishes. God gives us only the innocent hands of his Son with nails cruelly driven through at the wrists into the timbers of a cross. God gives us only the compassionate and scarred hands of the living Lord raised in a divine benediction over our lives.

Rejoice in God's mystery. Someday we will know that God's mystery is far greater than any magic, because the mystery of God is the great miracle of his divine mercy. There is a positive purpose in everything that happens in our lives. Trust God. Trust the miracle of his mysterious mercy. Trust — because there is a power, a peace, and a joy in that mysterious mercy of God that passes all human understanding.

Counterfeit Faith

Have you ever unintentionally passed a phony five dollar bill? According to the United States Treasury Department, you may have. And one of the reasons you may have is because a man by the name of Blinky was the greatest counterfeiter of all times. He made five dollar bills that defied detection. It was impossible, even for the experts, to identify the real bill from the counterfeit. It is estimated that hundreds, if not thousands, of the Blinky-made five dollar bills are still in circulation.

A bizarre set of circumstances finally led to Blinky's arrest and imprisonment. It seemed that he was so successful at counterfeiting five dollar bills that he decided to expand his operations. He started making twenty dollar bills. He was arrested while passing one of his phony twenties. In court, his lawyer followed the same line of defense; he challenged the experts to identify the phony bill from the real one. Immediately, the experts did so. Later Blinky discovered where he had made his tragic mistake. The bill that he had used to copy his counterfeit twenty was itself a counterfeit.

Our text this morning is about counterfeit faith — the counterfeit faith which Paul confronted in Lystra. According to the dictionary, the word "counterfeit" is defined as something made in imitation of something else. It is a fake or copy made to resemble the real or the genuine article. It is exactly that kind of faith that Paul and Barnabas experienced in the pagan city of Lystra.

Paul and Barnabas were on a missionary journey witnessing and preaching the Gospel of Jesus Christ. They had experienced both acceptance and rejection; but, they had no idea
of what was going to happen to them as they entered Lystra.
Immediately, a crowd gathered, and Paul began to preach.

Preachers are taught in the seminary that one begins a sermon where the listeners are — hitting a point of human in-
terest or a common concern. So, Paul begins his sermon talking
about the Creator God who made the heavens and the earth.
Lystra was a dry and arid country; so Paul stressed in the introduction to his sermon the fact that the God which he
represented was the God who sends the refreshing and life-
supporting rain.

The people listened intently. Then, seeing a man who was
crippled from birth, Paul stopped his sermon. In a loud voice
he cried out to the crippled man, "Arise, stand on your feet."
Immediately, the man leaped to his feet and began to walk.

At first, the people were stunned; but, then they suddenly
exploded with the excitement of a true conversion and started
to shout, "The gods have come down to us in the likeness of
men!" The people had witnessed a miracle, and they spontaneously began to celebrate. They decorated several bulls with
garlands of flowers and led them to the temple of Zeus to offer
sacrifice to the visiting divine dignitaries from heaven.

This spontaneous accolade to Paul and Barnabas, being
mistaken for gods, is easily understandable when we learn from
Roman historians of the time that there was an ancient legend
which was popular in the days when Paul and Barnabas made
their visit to Lystra. According to the legend, Zeus and Hermes,
disguised as mortals, had come to the region of Lystra some
years before. All except two people in the community rejected
them. The two gods, in turn, sent judgment on the area —
except for the old couple who had accepted and welcomed Zeus
and Hermes into their home. Because of this, the old couple
were made guardians of a magnificent temple on the out-skirts
of Lystra. When the old couple died, they were turned into

giant trees as living memorials for their kind reception of the gods. Perhaps it was under these very trees that Paul and Barnabas first preached.

There is little doubt that, when the people saw the miracle Paul performed, they remembered the legend, and they were certain that their visitors were gods in disguise. Barnabas with his white hair and muscular build was identified as Zeus, the head of the pantheon of pagan gods. Paul, because of his speaking skills, was declared to be Hermes, the god of eloquence and rhetoric.

The positive response of the people to Paul's preaching was really the reaction of a counterfeit faith. It was a faith-reaction, not resulting from the heard Word of God. It was the legacy of a legend. Paul never had the opportunity to get to the body of the sermon and to preach about Christ as the living Lord. The people's premature reaction was that of amazement to a miracle. Plus, it was an ingrained superstition that the gods played at the game of walking among men and women while masquerading as mortals. The people actually acted before they heard the Word of Christ proclaimed.

We sometimes say that a person's mouth races at ninety miles per hour before his or her mind is in gear. So, the people of Lystra went through the appearance of an excited faith before they had ever heard the Word that produces faith. That is why their faith was counterfeit. Because it was not born from the hearing of the Word, it was not genuine faith.

Last week we talked about the need of the heard Word becoming transformed into a life of faith. Today, we see the danger of a premature action — before the Word of God is fully and faithfully proclaimed. The people heard the nonverbals of the miracle that Paul performed. The words which they heard were the echoes of their own desires and fears. They heard in the miracle what they wanted to hear; therefore, their faith was self-initiated. And, self-initiated faith is counterfeit faith.

Today, we face the danger of counterfeit faith. We fail to

hear the Word of God because of preconceived or preestablished ideas of what we think is the word that God would speak. Frequently, that is why there is a vast gulf between what a preacher says in the pulpit and what the people hear in the pews. People have a built-in computer which is programmed to provide answers that have been fed into the computer before the question is asked. Like the prince in the story of Cinderella, who searched for the one foot that would fit the glass slipper, we have a glass slipper of expectations; and we will accept only those ideas about God which fit the slippers that we think are valid and reasonable.

Some of us, when we hear about the virgin birth, the miracles of healing, and the strange stories about Jesus stilling the storm, walking on water, and changing water into wine, attempt to dilute the miracle into some type of rational and scientific interpretation that fits our preestablished slipper of truth. However, when we do dilute a miracle, we actually dissolve it. To explain a miracle only results in explaining the miracle away. And, a faith without belief in miracles is, in the light of the New Testament, a counterfeit faith.

Many of us, when we hear that we are to love our neighbors, interpret the word "neighbor" to be people like ourselves, people who are the same as we are — the same social class, the same color, and the same economic status. We say to ourselves, "God really doesn't want us or expect us to love the hardened criminals in prisons, or the dirty and smelly street-people, or drunks, or prostitutes, or perverts." That extreme love does not fit into our conservative glass slipper. So, we limit "neighbor" to our own dimensions. And, when we do, our faith becomes counterfeit.

Surveys tell us that when most of the people in the Christian church today hear the good news about unmerited and unearned grace, they accept it only with a conditional "if." Many of us add an "if" to total grace. We think that God is a God of total grace — *if* we do something to deserve it. We are encouraged in this type of thinking by modern advertisements that continually speak of a "free gift" which will be sent to us "if." In Christian theology, such a phrase as a "free gift" is redundant. The New Testament knows of no gift of grace that is not *free*. If a gift costs something, then it is not a gift; it is a purchase paid for, or it becomes a service that is bought. Despite what the Bible proclaims, we still believe that one does not "get something for nothing," or "everything has its price," or "beware of Greeks bearing gifts." These are the glass slippers, fashioned by our "common sense," into which we attempt to force the foot of faith. When we do, the faith that we possess is not genuine. It is counterfeit. It does not fit the faith of the New Testament.

One of the greatest barriers to receiving the seed of God's Word in our lives is all the weeds that grow and flourish within us. Our minds and hearts are literally jungles of pseudo-scientific mind-sets, superstitious fears, and the bank of natural knowledge that we call "horse sense" (which, in most cases, is not very complimentary even to a horse). Tragically, most of our responses to God's revelation are not based on "horse sense" as much as they are an expression of our "bull-headedness." We hear only what we want to hear. We believe only what agrees with what we already believe. We accept only what fits our Cinderella slippers. As a result, we end up with a counterfeit faith.

It is interesting to note that if you read on in the Book of Acts beyond the limits of our text, you will discover that the people of Lystra, who at first hailed Paul and Barnabas as gods, soon completely changed and called them demons. They drove them from their city — stoning the preachers of Christ and leaving them for dead outside the city walls. But, that is another story. The story of our text is about fitting the Word of God into our own preconceived presuppositions and never hearing anything except what we want to hear.

Now, where is the Gospel — the good news in all of this? Is it not more discouraging and condemning than it is helpful and healing to hear about the counterfeit faith, which Paul and Barnabas encountered as they preached the Word about Christ Jesus? Perhaps, if we confine ourselves exclusively to this single text, there is no good news. However, the truth is that we do not have to limit ourselves to any one text, and the Book of Acts certainly does not limit its story to one event. The Book of Acts goes on to report that, despite the rejection and despite the counterfeit faith, the church of Jesus Christ grew, flourished, and established a beachhead in Europe that would eventually spread across the world.

God is not frustrated by counterfeit faith. He who healed the crippled man in Lystra can also cure the crippled minds that have been corrupted and twisted by counterfeit faith. God can, and will, harness and tame our bullheadedness. God can, and will, take our superstitions in his stride and change us into people who recognize the truth when we hear it. God will create people who honestly desire to hear what they *need* to hear rather than what they *want* to hear. God is still God, and our personal salvation still ultimately depends not on our faith — true or counterfeit. Our salvation, and the salvation of all people, depends on God's faith — God's faith in us — a faithfulness that will never surrender or accept defeat. God's faith is a faith that will persevere against all odds and win!

In the town of Livingston near Victoria Falls in Africa, there is a museum which holds the memorabilia of the missionary David Livingstone. One of the most prized and popular exhibits is a gold watch and chain worn by Dr. Livingstone. His close friends tell that each night before he went to bed, the last thing he would do was to wind his watch in preparation for his next day's work.

The night that he was told that he was dying and would more than likely not live through the night, Dr. Livingstone raised up on his elbow, reached for his gold watch, and carefully wound it as if preparing for another day's work.

In contrast to counterfeit faith, that was a true act of genuine faith. David Livingstone knew that with his death the Christianization of Africa would not end. It was not his work that would conquer Africa for Jesus Christ — rather, it was God's work. Even though Dr. Livingstone's efforts to serve Africa were at an end, God's efforts were not.

The faith of David Livingstone and his trust in the power of God is today vindicated by the fact that Christianity is growing more dramatically in Africa than on any other continent of the world.

Rejoice! The future of the church is not in our weak little hands. The church is in the all-powerful, never-tiring hands of God. The faith that saves us and our world is God's faith in us. This faith is not counterfeit: it is solid gold. Therefore, rejoice! Wind your watch — tomorrow belongs to God.

Acts 15:1-2, 22-29   *The Sixth Sunday of Easter*

No Grey Area

Our text this morning is about one of the greatest spiritual and theological events in the history of the Christian church. Interestingly enough, it was not a dramatic martyrdom, nor a mass miracle, or even a crusade. It was not a worship service, a great sermon preached, or a crowd conversion. It was a church convention — a convention held about fifty years after the death of our Lord.

For those of you who have ever attended a convention of the church, it may sound unbelievable that it could be a spiritual or a theological event. In many cases, for the neophyte minister or the layperson, one's first attendance at a church convention can be a shocking and even a faith-shaking experience. As one newly-ordained young minister was heard to say after his first day at convention, "If the Devil wants to destroy Christians, he should send them all as delegates to a church convention."

After all, the church is a human institution; of course, it is more than that — much more. But, the fact remains that the church is a human institution with all the frailties and faults of a political organization. There are caucuses that meet at night behind closed doors. There is the "good old boy" system where persons in power maneuver the meetings to keep the "young bucks" under control and to maintain safe middle-of-the-road policies. This results in the church following social trends rather than spearheading them. There is also "log rolling," where bargains are struck — "You vote for my motion, and I'll vote for yours." All of this is present — all of this and more.

Nevertheless, the truth is that the Holy Spirit works better in the corporate context of a convention or at a council meeting than he does in isolated individuals who claim that God has spoken to them privately and personally and has given them an exclusive revelation. The guidance of the Holy Spirit thrives best in the conflict of publicly-expressed opinions, where people meet together and struggle, honestly and openly, with various biblical interpretations, theology, the mission, and the business of the church.

This was the case in our text for today. The apostolic convention, which was held at Jerusalem, was marked by strong differences of opinion and heated debates. Here was Paul's first sharp clash with the Judaizers, and Barnabas stood staunchly at his side. Peter was also there, and the spotlight of our text falls directly upon him. The issue at stake was crucial for the future of the church. The issue was: "What are the essential requirements for a person to be saved?"

The Judaizers stood firm in their conviction that, first and foremost, for a Gentile to become a Christian, he had first to become a Jew. Their slogan was: "Unless you are circumcised according to the custom of Moses, you cannot be saved." It was not the physical act of circumcision that concerned them as much as it was that circumcision was a symbol of the old covenant of the law. Faced with the glories of the new covenant, the Judaizers were not willing to let go of the glories of the old law-covenant. Faith in Christ was not enough to save a person; something had to be added — the rite of circumcision and the holy legacy of the law.

In contrast to a combination of the old and the new covenants and a blending of faith in Christ with obedience to the law, Peter and Paul and their followers stood steadfast in their conviction that it was Christ, and Christ alone, who saves. To add any requirements to faith in Christ as necessary to attain salvation — even participation in the sacraments of baptism and communion, or acts of confession and penitence — weakens the power of the cross and places limitations on Christ as our total savior. If a bridge to heaven has only one rivet of human steel to hold two beams together, under pressure and stress, it will break down at this joint; it will cease to be a bridge at all. As one scholar put it, "Even if Christ be conceived as carrying us 599 miles on the way to the throne of God, anything merely human for the last mile would drop us all crashingly into the depths of hell."

The theological temptation to interject added requirements to the pure, the simple, and the direct doctrine of justification by Christ, and by Christ alone, is not limited to the ancient church. We face the same fatal heresy today. Well-intentioned and biblically knowledgeable people claim that a particular and an exclusive manner of baptism is necessary for salvation. Others claim that a second baptism by the Holy Spirit is an absolute must for "born again" salvation. Others stake salvation on the possession of charismatic gifts, public confessions of faith, penitence, and absolution by the church. The list goes on and on. Such attempts to add such baggage to the doctrine of salvation by Christ, and by Christ alone, causes Saint Peter, in our text for this morning, to shout out a sharply pointed warning, "Why are you tempting God, to place a yoke upon the neck of the disciples which neither our fathers nor we were strong enough to bear?"

The phrase used here — "tempting God" — is an interesting one. As Peter uses it, it means to tease or to challenge God by adding additional requirements to his act of salvation in Jesus Christ. Tempting God means to test God to see whether God will overlook this deliberate altering of his intended purpose to save the world by means of the cross — and the cross alone. Will God resent these additions to the cross-event and punish the offenders? It is much like mischievous students who play pranks and test a new teacher to see how much devilishment they can get away with without being punished. So, Peter warns the Judaizers. They are playing pranks with God. They are testing God's patience with their human additions to his revealed plan of redemption through Jesus Christ — and through Jesus Christ alone!

In the New Testament, salvation is best summarized by the word "freedom." Christ sets us free — free from the law; free from ritual, rules, and regulations; free from self-centered lives; free from sin, death, and the Devil. It is human-sided religion that burdens us with the yokes of liturgies and laws, rules and regulations.

The fifteenth chapter of Acts tells us that, for a time, the council at Jerusalem succeeded in silencing the yoke-builders and those who would play God by adding their own amendments to the revelation of the Gospel of Christ. It was not to last (but, that is another story).

At the end of the convention, the various warring factions were united. However, this unity was not to last. The struggle for unity is a constant battle. Therefore, we need to look briefly at how unity was achieved, for a time, in the early church. There were basically five factors which marked the procedure that accomplished unity in that church convention which was held about fifty years after the death of our Lord.

First, despite their differences, they agreed to meet together in order to talk to each other, because they all accepted Jesus Christ as their Lord and their savior. The horizontal and the vertical dimensions of the beams of the cross symbolize the possibility of diversity within an overall unity.

Second, they did not deny their differences. We frequently think that the sign of unity and fellowship is when everyone agrees on everything. The truth is, true fellowship is being able to attack and to argue issues without attacking and tearing down the people who hold conflicting ideas. Lawyers, more than any other professionals, are excellent examples of this. They can fight like gladiators in the arena of the court room; but, during the noon adjournment, they can lunch together as if life-long friends.

Third, the delegates at the Jerusalem Council apparently listened to each other. How often communication between people breaks down because they do not listen to each other. Our minds are not on what *the speaker* is saying; rather, our minds are concentrating on what *we* are going to say, once we gain the floor and have the opportunity to speak.

Fourth, the convention at Jerusalem was open to the judgment and the guidance of the Holy Spirit. At every gathering of the church, there are always the number of people who are attending the meeting — plus *one* — and that one is God, himself, present in the Holy Spirit.

Fifth, they did not conclude or close the convention at Jerusalem until a consensus of common agreement was reached. Unity in the Spirit demands persistence and patience. Any disagreement can be solved if we are willing to give the time and the attention to it which it demands.

These five factors form an excellent pattern for the solving of differences in any convention or meeting of the church. And, we might add, they are the basic ingredients in the solving of family disputes or hassles between friends. The acceptance of Christ as Lord, debating issues, not debasing people, listening, and being open to the guidance of the Holy Spirit through patience and persistence — these ingredients are the way to unity and solidarity for all, who would claim to be a part of the Body of Christ.

A legend tells us of two knights in armor who were riding down a road. They passed a shield which was hanging from a tree. They both stopped. One said, "Did you see that magnificent white shield hanging from the tree?" "I did," the other knight answered, "but, it was black." "You are color blind," shouted the first knight. "I am certain that it was white."

The debate became so heated that they climbed down from their horses and began dueling with their swords. A monk, who was passing by saw the fierce fight and stepped between them. After listening to their opposite opinions as to the color of the shield, the old monk smiled, as one possessing great wisdom, and said, "Good gentlemen, let us strike a compromise. Let us agree that the shield was not pure white or pure black; rather, it was a delicate shade of gray, which one of you saw as white in the sunlight and the other saw as black in the shadows."

The knights, overcome by such wise insight, agreed. All three men went their merry ways — and all of them were dead wrong. For the truth was that the knights had passed the shield on opposite sides, and the shield was black on one side and white on the other.

So, the shield of faith is black on one side and white on the other. The black side of faith is the Law. It was given to us by God — not to save us, but to prepare us for salvation. The Law is a mirror that reflects how far short we have fallen from God's intention for our lives. The Law makes us aware that we cannot, by our own efforts, obey God's will, fulfill his demands, or measure up to his standards. The Law is intended to bring us to a state of total helplessness where we are certain that we can do nothing — absolutely nothing — to accomplish our own salvation. We are helpless!

The white side of the shield of faith is the Gospel. The Gospel proclaims that, in our state of total helplessness, there is hope. God's grace is sufficient. Christ, and Christ alone, saves us and gives us a new and a transformed life.

There is no grey area between the Law and the Gospel. The Law prepares. The Gospel alone saves. The Law must be pure as the Gospel is pure. Such is the plan and the purpose of God. To add laws and requirements to the process of salvation by Christ, and Christ alone, is to compromise the cross (settle for the wisdom of the world) and to live in a state of grey togetherness — rather than walking as one in the light of Christ.

Therefore, rejoice. Law and Gospel are both expressions of God's determination to save us; but, they must never be confused. The Law must be pure, just as the Gospel is pure. The Law is important, but it is the Gospel that alone saves us from our sins and grants us a new life by grace.

We are off to the convention. The banner of the Father's shield of faith waves over us. The cross of Christ leads the procession. The Holy Spirit is at work within us. We are one — united in the Body of Christ. Three cheers for the church of the Father, the Son, and the Holy Spirit!

Jail House Joy

You may, or you may not be a fan of Elvis Presley. Fans or not, most people agree that he was the King of Rock and Roll. When Elvis shook his hips, the public was shocked. His gyrations vibrated the public's moral standards and dislodged them from their conservative moorings. He opened a door that cannot be easily closed. Things, once held as strictly private, became openly public. Critics tell us that his most innovative song was entitled "Jail House Rock." Up until this time, "blues" had been associated with imprisonment. Elvis brought joy into the jail house.

Now, you are probably wondering what all this has to do with the text today. More than likely, you hope the answer is "Nothing!" However, the truth is that this is a direct lead-in to our text. The passage from Acts, read as our First Lesson, has to do with a man named Paul. He also shocked the public with his actions. He, too, radically dislodged culture from its historic moorings. Certainly not in the same direction as Elvis did it; but Paul ushered in a change in the culture of his day. The change Paul wrought was like that of Elvis Presley's song — the discovery of joy in a jail house.

If we jump into the middle of our text, we see two men, Paul and Silas, jailed behind stone walls and iron bars. They are singing. They are not singing "jail house blues"; rather, they are praising God by singing glorious hymns of joy. The jailors were shocked. Never before had such a thing been heard of — joy in a jail house, prisoners singing.

Now, why? How could Paul and Silas find the spirit to sing in jail? To answer this question, we need to examine what happened to Paul and Silas before they were jailed and what happened to them during and after their imprisonment. To do this, we need to look at the total text. It is a long and an involved story. It possesses all of the elements of an afternoon television soap opera; there is a slave girl with a touch of insanity, who is a soothsayer; there are con-men, who exploit her; there is racial prejudice; there is an imprisonment; there is an earthquake; there is an attempted suicide which turns into a religious conversion.

But, let us start at the beginning. Paul and Silas have attended the church convention which we spoke of in the sermon last Sunday. They are returning to their missionary work. Their first stop is the Roman colony at Philippi. Few Jews lived there; and those who did were not wanted. Anti-semitism ran rampant. Since there was no synagogue in Philippi, Paul and Silas preached to a small group of women at a riverbank prayer meeting. One woman, named Lydia, was converted. She, along with her whole family, was baptized.

After this less-than-smashing success, Paul and Silas entered the city. Instantly, they were the center of attention. This was not because of their preaching; it was because of the fact that they were pursued by a demonically-possessed fortune teller, who followed after them everywhere, crying out, "These men are servants of the most high God who proclaimed to us the way of salvation."

This attracted attention and also gave Paul and Silas plenty of free publicity. But it would seem to us, that it was publicity that Paul and Silas could have done better without. To us, an insane slave girl screaming in the streets, is not the best means of establishing good public relations. To us, it would be like seeing your picture and name on the cover of the *National Enquirer* or some other scandal sheet. However, this was not the case in the days of Paul. At that time, it was believed that when a person lost his or her mental faculties, it meant that the gods had invaded the person and that the gods proclaimed predictions of the future through that person.

What the insane girl was saying was true. However, her words were not inspired by God. Rather, they were directed by the Evil One, who was cunningly attempting to gain control of the situation and to discredit the effects of the witnessing of Paul and Silas.

Paul, however, was able to discern the difference between the words of a demonically-possessed fortune teller and the authentic proclamation of one who had been blessed with a gift of prophecy from the Holy Spirit. So, Paul turned to the deranged girl and, on the spot, performed a miracle of exorcism which drove the demon from her. What Paul did *not* know, but what he was soon to find out, was that the conmen in the city, those who owned the slave girl, were making a handsome profit from her prophesying. They were outraged by their sudden loss of revenue. So, they had Paul and Silas arrested and taken into court by charging them with inciting a riot. All the judge had to hear was that they were Jews, and his prejudice prompted him to exercise "the" appropriate justice — immediately! He ordered them to be stripped, to be beaten, and to be thrown into prison. That is the first act of the drama which is recorded in our text. The second act begins with Paul and Silas as they are confined to jail. Ironically, they are in jail not because they had been preaching Christ, but rather because they had been born Jews.

It was midnight. In the damp darkness of their cell, even though their legs and arms were in chains, their lips were free. They sang hymns of joy and praise to God. Their voices echoed and re-echoed through the halls of the Roman jailhouse. The prison guard, who was awakened from his sleep by the singing, thought to himself that they were making the very walls vibrate — and the floor and the doors. Suddenly he realized that it was not the singing that was causing the lantern above him to swing. It was an earthquake! The very foundation of the prison was shaken. The locks of the doors sprung open. The iron gates burst loose from the beams. The bolts in the walls fell out and no longer held the chains. The prisoners were free.

When the jailor saw that his prisoners had escaped, he panicked. He knew that a long and lingering torture would be his punishment for permitting the prisoners to escape. So, he drew his short sword and was ready to commit suicide. This was preferable to facing a severe and an agonizing death at the hands of his superiors. Paul cried out to him, "Do not harm yourself, for we are here!" The jailor looked up and saw that the other freed prisoners had not run away. They were standing around Paul and Silas. Though set free, they did not flee.

The jailor fell to his knees in front of Paul. An inner earthquake shook the very foundation of his being and he cried out to Paul, "What must I do to be saved?" He received the answer: "Believe in the Lord Jesus Christ, and you will be saved, you and your household." The jailor confessed. Soon thereafter, he and all of his family were baptized.

Beyond the limits of our established text, there was a third act to the drama of our text yet to be played out. This third act tells us that the jailor, his family, Lydia and her family; and the freed prisoners formed the nucleus of a strong church which grew and flourished. It was to this same church that Paul wrote the Epistle to the Philippians, which expressed so much tender love and encouragement. Out of great adversity and persecution God brought great blessings. The earth was still quaking from the resurrection; Jesus Christ, the crucified one, was becoming the cornerstone of an edifice — the church, which would change the course of history and decide the destiny of millions.

Why, or how, could Paul and Silas sing hymns of praise and joy in a Philippian jail house? They could sing, because they were, before all else, prisoners of Christ. And to be captured by Christ, is to know a freedom that cannot be fettered by anything in all of life. For to be in Christ, is to add a dimension to the height of all of life that no ceiling can limit, no walls can enclose, and no iron bars can confine.

Dr. Grensted of Oxford University was a giant of the faith. When he wrote about Jesus Christ, he added a range to redemption that challenges the horizons of human imagination. When he lectured, the spectrum of his thoughts expanded the minds of his students to the limits of their capacities. Long before the first moon landing, Dr. Grensted had traveled into the outer space of faith — giving Christ cosmic dimensions.

Frequently in his lectures, Dr. Grensted would mention the spaciousness of his garden where he worked, wrote, and prepared his lectures. One day, several of his students were invited to take tea in Dr. Grensted's garden. When they entered the gates to the garden, they expected to see acres of trees, shrubs, vast lawns, and flower beds. They were shocked. Instead, they found a tiny, little, walled-in garden no more than twelve feet square.

Seeing the shock on the faces of his students, the old professor remarked, "You are surprised at the smallness of my garden. True, it is not very long, and it is not very wide; but, just look up. There is no limit to the height of my garden. It reaches up to the very heart of God in heaven."

Prisons that enslave people and their minds have walls, floors, and ceilings. However, it is the ceilings that truly imprison us. Paul was constantly referring to himself as a prisoner of the love and the grace of Christ. But he could sing hymns of joy and praise to God because the prison of Christ has no ceiling. Once you have committed your life to Christ, your life takes on a dimension of height that reaches into the very heart of God in heaven.

You may feel fenced in by life. Tragic circumstances and troubles may erect stone walls around you. Distress and depression may forge iron bars across the windows of your life. But rejoice, because in Jesus Christ nothing in all the world can create a ceiling to separate you from the love of God. Nothing in all the world can limit the height of your life. In Christ Jesus, life is as high as heaven itself. Therefore, sing with Paul and Silas. Rejoice and sing. Let the whole world rock and roll with praises to God. Amen!

The Same New Jesus

In most Christian churches Ascension Day is "A Silent Day." The church doors are closed and locked. The nave is empty. The pulpit and the choir loft are unoccupied. The candles on the altar are topped with charred wicks, indicating that worship has happened here in the past, but is in no way happening now.

It is curious that we so easily confess the Ascension in our creeds, but we have great difficulty in celebrating it in our churches. Perhaps, this is due to the fact that Ascension is tucked away on a weekday and we are Sunday-only worshipers.

It may be that our neglect of the Ascension story is due to the fact that it is dependent on a world view which we have long ago discarded. The idea that Jesus ascended, like a rocket launched into outer space, and landed on a celestial satellite — a space station in the sky called heaven — and that Christ sits there in a chair at the right hand of God, is just too fantastic for us to believe. A crucifixion is believable. A resurrection is unusual, but not unbelievable (particularly when we *want* to believe it, for the sake of our own destiny after death). However, a tale about a man, floating upward into the clouds sounds more like the levitation of a magic show than it does a revelation from God.

In the creed, when we refer to the Ascension of our Lord, we confess that "He ascended into heaven, and sitteth at the right hand of God . . ." We are not witnessing to the physical fact that God has a right hand, nor are we saying that there is a chair that is suspended in outer space where our Lord sits beside the throne of God. This is picture language, used by believers to confess the conviction that the same Jesus who puts aside his might and majesty to be born a baby in a Bethlehem barn, now, once more, assumes his position of power as the Son of God and the Lord of all creation.

Picture language is not unusual. We say that the sun "rises or sets," knowing full well that the sun does not literally rise in the East and set in the West. It is the earth that moves, not the sun. However, such picture language communicates accurately what we experience. When the writers of the New Testament desired to picture for us what the disciples had experienced as the Son returned to the Father; they said that he ascended into the clouds and above the clouds into heaven. There he reigns in power with God the Father.

To argue the historic factuality of the Ascension-event is not to achieve a more accurate communication of revelation, but to distort it. In the end we miss completely what God, through the sacred record of the Bible, is trying to say to us. God does not desire to prove that he can defy the law of gravity, nor is he identifying the location of heaven in the sky — or in outer space. God is not trying to hide something with the clouds that surrounded our Lord at his Ascension; rather, God desires to clarify and to verify what happened to Jesus after his resurrection. Our Lord was neither time-bound nor space-bound by his resurrection body. Rather, he was released to reign as sovereign king of all creation. His presence and his power are unlimited. This profound revelation cannot be communicated without the ascension imagery of a movement *upward*. Christ was moving upward to a higher level of life — a life that was higher than the tangible, material, localized, and limited life that we know.

The intent of the Ascension was to reveal to the apostles and to us that Jesus was moving up to a new mode of existence and activity. He was not only raised from death; he was raised up from this space-bound, time-bound life to reign eternally in glory.

By failing to understand the intent of the Ascension, we risk forgetting the festival because it has become a dead doctrine for us. If so, it is essential for the full force of our redemption experience to revive it. The Ascension means many things, but basically the meaning of the Ascension-event can be summarized in three words: confirmation, extension, and coronation.

•First, the meaning of the Ascension is the *confirmation* of our Lord. Without Christmas, there would be no Cross. Without Easter, the Cross would be a meaningless martyrdom. Without the Ascension, Easter would be a victory without verification. The Ascension is our Lord's confirmation by God the Father. As he was baptized by the Cross and Resurrection, he is now confirmed by the Ascension. God the Father confirms and verifies his acceptance of all Christ has done for us. Our Lord's ministry of obedience and the sacrificial offering of his death for our sins have been accepted by God the Father. We are accepted by his acceptance.

We need to know not only what happened to Jesus through the event of the Ascension but also *what happens to us because of it.* Our status of being restored to the family of God is confirmed by the Ascension. Our status as born-again children of God is confirmed by the Ascension. As the early church fathers put it, "Christ became what we are in order that we might become what he is."

But more! The Ascension assures us that Christ is our eternal advocate — our "defense attorney." When the Evil One stands and accuses us of sins in the court of God, Christ intercedes for us. Our Lord pleads our innocence based on his sacrifice on Calvary for our sins. He covers us with the innocence of his righteousness. Seminary professor C. George Fry graphically reminds us that, when Christ is our lawyer, the "anxious bench" of guilt and the "mourner's bench" of repentance are transformed into the "mercy seat" of joy!

•The second word of the Ascension event is *extension*. Without the good news of the Ascension, our relationship to the Lord would be limited to hearing the story of the earthly Jesus. It would be second-hand information at best. However, the Ascension proclaims the extension of Christ beyond the limitations of time and space. Now we can have direct access with the ascended Lord.

The phrase, "at the right hand of God," does not locate a place. It refers to an act of participation. Christ participates not only with the sovereignty of God over all things; he also, and at the same time, participates in the lives of all believers. As he sits at the right hand of God, our Lord's hands can still reach into our lives and touch us. Christ is present to wipe away our tears and to penetrate the loneliness of our lives with his Joy-filled presence.

•*Confirmation* of our acceptance by God the Father, *extension* of our Lord's presence into our lives; finally, the Ascension means *coronation*. The Ascension crowns our Lord with glory, majesty, and power. It is one thing to assert that Jesus has been raised from death; it is quite another thing to assert that he now shares the sovereignty of God over heaven and earth.

Most of our thinking about Christ is in the single dimension of his common humanity — a babe born in a barn, a friend of fishermen, a rural rabbi who walked the dusty back-roads of Palestine, wearing a homespun robe, quietly teaching the truths about God, challenging the pride of the Pharisees, discouraging the elaborate ritual of the priests and the liturgical extravagancies of the temple.

We picture our Lord as the "Gentle Jesus," the humble "Servant-Savior" with a bowl and a towel, who sits washing the feet of his disciples and silently submitting to the ignominious death of a criminal on a cross. This is a true picture of our Lord, but, it is only a one-dimensional view. It is only a partial picture of our Lord, particularly when we fail to project our vision above time and space in order to catch a vision of the regal Christ who reigns as king of all creation.

The evidence of the Ascension is limited in the New Testament. Only the Book of Acts gives a detailed account. But, what the Ascension of our Lord symbolizes and stands for is — the *confirmation* of our acceptance by God, the *extension* of our Lord's presence into our daily lives, the *coronation* of Christ as king of all creation. All of this permeates to the heart of every word penned by the writers of the New Testament. These inspired believers, who wrote the words of Holy Scripture, were men who were enlightened and lifted up by the risen and the ascended Lord. The perspective of the Ascension is the viewpoint from which they witnessed. They wrote, not with fear-filled hearts and tear-filled eyes. Rather, they sang each word that they wrote with the hope and the joy which was flooding every fiber of their being. They had caught the vision of the ultimate victory of Christ. They were messengers of a battle fought and won — and of a kingdom come. They saw beyond the man, Jesus, to Christ the King. They saw beyond the stable to the sacred sanctuary of God. They saw beyond the cross to the crown. They saw beyond the tomb to the ultimate triumph.

Across the street from our seminary stands Ascension Lutheran Church. Above the altar is a stained glass window which depicts the ascending Christ. The congregation decided to completely remodel the chancel of the church. Because of the sentimental attachment of the people to the altar window, they decided to retain the ascension window in the new design.

When the remodeling was completed and the congregation returned to the church for worship, the little seven-year-old son of the pastor leaned over to his mother and said, "A brand new church, but the same old Jesus."

Now, it is true that Jesus is old. He is, in fact, one thousand nine hundred and eighty-nine years old. He is historically removed from us by nearly two centuries. We remind ourselves of this fact every time that we date a check, begin a letter, or ask someone what day it is. Yet, the good news of the

Ascension is that Jesus Christ is both old and new. On the one hand, he is the same "old Jesus" but, on the other hand, he is the same "new Jesus" — new every day, because his acts of power are not limited to the record of his earthly life. The Holy Spirit brings Christ to us daily in his "real presence."

The message of the Ascension — the *confirmation* of our acceptance by God, the *extension* of our Lord's presence in our lives, and the *coronation* of his kingly power over all creation — can be condensed to one simple truth; "Christ is Lord and he is with us." The same Christ who lived and died, the same Christ who was resurrected and ascended in kingly power is our daily companion and friend, our daily defender and protector. Rejoice! Christ lives forever in us, with us, and for us. We are strengthened by his power. We are engulfed by his glory.

We are truly alive in him, and he is alive in us.

About the Author

The Reverend Dr. Richard Carl Hoefler, Dean of Christ Chapel, professor of preaching at the Lutheran Theological Southern Seminary, Columbia, South Carolina was graduated with an A.B. degree from Wittenberg University and received his M.Div. degree from Wittenberg University in 1945.

Dr. Hoefler was then pastor at St. John's Lutheran Church, Springfield, Ohio for four years, at which time he was also instructor of Bible and Speech at Wittenberg University.

Dr. Hoefler then studied at Oxford University, England for his B.Litt. degree. Returning to America, he became a professor of Bible at Wittenberg University. In 1953 he attended Princeton Seminary and received his M.Th. degree.

Dr. Hoefler has done graduate studies at the University of London, The University of Paris, Columbia University and Union Theological Seminary in New York.

In 1977 Milton Crum, Jr., Professor of Homiletics at the Episcopal Seminary, Virginia, dedicated his book *Manual on Preaching,* to Professor Hoefler "who taught me to preach."

Dr. Hoefler is the author of the following books:

Creative Preaching
And He Told Them A Story
There Are Demons In The Sea
Will Daylight Come?
The Divine Trap
I Knew You'd Come
A Sign In The Straw
Realize and Rejoice
At Noon On Friday
With Wings Of Eagles

www.ingramcontent.com/pod-product-compliance
Lightning Source LLC
LaVergne TN
LVHW051655080426

835511LV00017B/2588

* 9 7 8 1 5 5 6 7 3 0 5 9 7 *